King gives a stirring and convincing defense [...]
it gets even better than this because King exp[...]
Testament. Preachers are busy, and it is difficul[...]
however, is succinct and marvelously clear. Take up and read!

THOMAS R. SCHREINER, James Buchanan Harrison Professor of New Testament Interpretation, Associate Dean, The Southern Baptist Theological Seminary, Louisville, KY

This short book bears the marks of a long gestation. Its brevity is owing to years of faithful preaching and careful thought about preaching. It is clear, to the point, and ideal for reading as you come up for air between sermons. Here you'll find a guide to genuinely preach Christ from the Old Testament, alongside a warning against narrowness, quickness, and laziness. Both are needed. David King has weathered the pendulum swings of moralism and gospelism, and he presses us both to help our people see Christ and to not "elbow the text out of the way" or be loose with the details of the passage. To preach a freer holiness, and a holier freedom. Here is an invitation, and accessible guide, into the journey of preaching the whole Bible to the whole church for a whole lifetime.

DAVID MATHIS, executive editor and senior teacher, desiringGod.org; pastor, Cities Church, Saint Paul; author, *Habits of Grace: Enjoying Jesus through the Spiritual Disciplines*

This practical handbook fills a much-needed gap in the recent discussions on Christ-centered preaching. It offers a compelling, robust, and balanced Christ-centered hermeneutic that does not overshadow the essential nature of the triune God as Father, Son, and Spirit.

JACOB M. PRATT, Assistant Professor of New Testament and Hermeneutics, Southeastern Baptist Theological Seminary

David King is an experienced, competent preaching pastor. This volume is a pastor speaking to pastors using the language of a pastor. Every preaching and teaching pastor will gain insights and practical guidance in bridging the message of the testaments. He rightly shows that the connection between the testaments is not one model "fits all" but different interpretative patterns according to the kind of specific OT passages. He shows how preaching Christ in the OT can be achieved without sacrificing the original message in the OT's historical and theological contexts. The volume's teaching is plainly presented and is clearly explained. As a handbook to preaching Christ from the OT, it will make a significant contribution to every preacher's wrestling with this critical question in the life of a preacher.

KENNETH A. MATHEWS, Professor of Divinity, Old Testament, Beeson Divinity School

Your Old Testament Needs to Get Saved offers a faithful strategy for moving from *reading* the Hebrew Bible to *heralding* the Old Testament as thirty-nine books revealing Jesus as the Christ. Those seeking a means of *discerning* Christ on every page of Scripture and *proclaiming* His lordship from all the Law and Prophets will find a strong theological and methodological approach contained herein. Gospel preachers will enjoy this work.

ERIC C. REDMOND, Professor of Bible, Moody Bible Institute

Following the pattern of Jesus in Luke 24, Pastor King shows us how to preach the Old Testament with the person and work of Christ constantly in view. As a wise pastor, King shows us why we should preach from the Old Testament, and how to do so. He also helps the reader understand the kinds of problems one should avoid when preaching from the Old Testament, as well as the benefits one derives from preaching this portion of Holy Scripture. I will be handing out *Your Old Testament Sermon Needs to Get Saved* to many others in hopes that we may saturate churches among the nations with the good news revealed in all of Scripture.

TONY MERIDA, Pastor for Preaching, Imago Dei Church, Raleigh, NC; Dean of Grimké Seminary; author, *The Christ-Centered Expositor*

Twenty-first century preaching, at least for evangelicals, has seen a renewed interest in preaching Christ from the whole Bible. What David King does in this handbook is provide the working pastor with a unified method for getting it done, and getting it done well. Drawing on the good work of others, he gives those of us who preach solid stuff and a simple approach. This work will help many.

DAVID HELM, Senior Pastor, Christ Church Chicago; chairman, The Charles Simeon Trust

David King has given preachers a gift in this book. It is comprehensive enough to be persuasive and clear enough to be practiced. This is a book that is as approachable as helpful for both preacher and parishioner alike. King is honest about his own failings in preaching Christ from the Old Testament. He thus comes across as a repentant practitioner coming alongside those who will hopefully become like him in the serious and surprising task of preaching like a Christian. King scatters practical examples throughout that demonstrate how to connect to the gospel in preaching, helping the reader understand how this all might actually work in preaching. He raises potential problems with simplistic and poor understandings of how to do this work and how to avoid them, leading to preaching that is better, not just different. As a preacher who is also an ethicist I was particularly encouraged by King's insistence that we do not connect to the gospel to eradicate, but rather encourage, obedient discipleship.

JEREMY MEEKS, Director, The Chicago Course on Preaching; host, *Preachers Talk* podcast

Christians are people of one book, but sometimes forget that the Bible they love has two testaments. Those who preach can be similarly one-sided, preferring to stick to the more familiar landscape of the New Testament and neglecting the Old. Others find it hard to reconcile the two, so that their Old Testament sermons either connect awkwardly to Jesus Christ or ignore Him altogether. In this book David M. King offers concise and helpful advice to help you to preach Christ from the Old Testament. He will both persuade you of the need and show you how to begin. I highly recommend it.

JOHN KOESSLER, general editor of *The Moody Handbook of Preaching* and author of *Folly, Grace, and Power: The Mysterious Act of Preaching*

This is an excellent resource for all pastors! If you are not sure about preaching Christ from the OT, David King will help you see why this is necessary, valuable to your people, and possible for you. If you are already convinced that you should preach Christ from the OT, King will provide you with a very accessible guide to achieving this goal consistently and faithfully. And, this is a book for preachers, from an experienced preacher and pastor. His empathy for those engaged in this significant task is clear, and he gets right to the heart of the issue in practical terms. His pastoral heart also comes through, guiding the reader to care faithfully for the flock by preaching Christ to them from all the Bible. This may be the most helpful book you could read on preaching this year.

RAY VAN NESTE, Dean of the School of Theology & Missions, Union University

While there is much being said and written these days about preaching Christ from all of Scripture, there is not as much being offered about exactly how to do it. We preachers need help, and David King's book provides a clear way forward. The self-announced aim of the book is the provision of a simple and practical methodology. The quality of a book is measured by the value of its aim and its effectiveness in accomplishing it. King's book scores high on both points. While one still wants to preserve the importance of preaching the doxological and ethical force of Scripture, King reminds us it is dangerous, even a failure of duty, to do so apart from the all-encompassing Word of Christ.

MIKE BULLMORE, Senior Pastor, CrossWay Community Church, Bristol, WI; founding member of The Gospel Coalition

YOUR OLD TESTAMENT SERMON NEEDS TO GET SAVED

A HANDBOOK FOR PREACHING CHRIST FROM THE OLD TESTAMENT

DAVID M. KING

MOODY PUBLISHERS

CHICAGO

© 2021 by
DAVID M. KING

Some content in chapter 6 was previously published on 9Marks.org: David King, "How (Not) to Preach the Pentateuch," March 31, 2020.

Edited by Kevin Mungons
Interior design: Ragont Design
Cover design: Erik M. Peterson

Library of Congress Cataloging-in-Publication Data

Names: King, David M., author.
Title: Your Old Testament sermon needs to get saved : a handbook for
  preaching Christ from the Old Testament / by David M. King.
Description: Chicago, IL : Moody Publishers, [2021] | Includes
  bibliographical references and index. | Summary: "Your Old Testament
  Sermon Needs to Get Saved is a practical handbook for preaching Christ
  from the Old Testament. You'll learn why and how to preach Christ from
  the Old Testament while experiencing the beauty of discovering and
  teaching how the saving work of Christ permeates the first two-thirds of
  the Bible"-- Provided by publisher.
Identifiers: LCCN 2020056668 (print) | LCCN 2020056669 (ebook) | ISBN
  9780802423276 (paperback) | ISBN 9780802499554 (ebook)
Subjects: LCSH: Bible. Old Testament--Homiletical use. | Preaching. |
  Typology (Theology) | Jesus Christ--Biblical teaching.
Classification: LCC BS1191.5 .K56 2021 (print) | LCC BS1191.5 (ebook) |
  DDC 251--dc23
LC record available at https://lccn.loc.gov/2020056668
LC ebook record available at https://lccn.loc.gov/2020056669

Originally delivered by fleets of horse-drawn wagons, the affordable paperbacks from D. L. Moody's publishing house resourced the church and served everyday people. Now, after more than 125 years of publishing and ministry, Moody Publishers' mission remains the same—even if our delivery systems have changed a bit. For more information on other books (and resources) created from a biblical perspective, go to www.moodypublishers.com or write to:

Moody Publishers
820 N. LaSalle Boulevard
Chicago, IL 60610

1 3 5 7 9 10 8 6 4 2

Printed in the United States of America

To Sidney, Graeme, and Bryan,
who were among the first to take my fragmented Bible
and hand it back to me whole.

Contents

The Rock in My Shoe

W hat thickheaded preacher would fail to observe Jesus' own Christ-centered approach to the Scriptures? What obtuse interpreter would overlook how the apostles virtually fasten themselves to the Bible in proclaiming Jesus as the Christ?

HERE I AM!

I was that thickheaded preacher. For nearly a decade of my pastoral ministry, I neglected Jesus in my Old Testament preaching. My neglect wasn't intentional. In fact, I often concluded my Old Testament sermons by talking about Jesus, feeling the need to preach Christ even when the text didn't appear to have anything to do with Him. But I hadn't yet perceived the Christocentric nature of the Old Testament.

Then one day, a perceptive old man put a rock in my shoe. At some point, he said, you must ask yourself, "How does the centrality of Jesus Christ affect the way that I handle the biblical texts? If a thoughtful Muslim or a Jew would be satisfied with my interpretation of the Old Testament, could it really be Christian?"[1] The question bothered me. I couldn't ignore it. I realized that the issue of preaching Christ from the Old Testament needed to be addressed at the hermeneutical level, not merely at the homiletical level. Surely Jesus has something to do with the text itself! And so it would no longer suffice to exposit the text apart from Christ, only to tack Him on to the end of my sermon.

Many Christian preachers have had this same rock in their shoe. They've felt the logical force of the Christocentric question and have concluded that preaching Christ from the Old Testament is necessary. However, the way forward remains unclear. Good intentions don't automatically yield sound interpretation.

Getting this right is no trifling matter. If a preacher fails to interpret and apply the Old Testament in light of Christ, his Old Testament preaching will inevitably be sub-Christian. Practically speaking, he may exalt God, commend faith, and encourage holy living, but do so without any explicit connection to Jesus and the gospel. Such a sermon is fit for the synagogue. It's a message for the mosque. More significantly, the preacher will have withheld from his hearers their only means of access to God. God's pardon of sin, His power for obedience, and His presence through the Holy Spirit come only through Jesus.

On the other hand, if a preacher carelessly applies a Christ-centered hermeneutic to the Old Testament, other problems will result. In his zeal to preach Christ, he may inadvertently slight the triune nature of God, or twist the Scriptures to get to Jesus, or minimize the ethical implications of the text. Rather than sub-Christian, this type of preaching is sub-biblical in that it disregards Scripture as inspired literature.

The Bible isn't mere literature, as it's sometimes taught in universities and liberal seminaries. But the Bible *is* literature. God communicates with us not through vague impressions but through words and sentences and paragraphs. He speaks intelligibly and precisely, marshalling a beautiful array of genres to do so. With the help of His Spirit, we can understand what is written. Appreciating the literary nature of God's revelation will guard the preacher from neglecting the details of the text in an effort to get to Jesus.

So the stakes are high. Whether the error is *no* Christocentric interpretation or *poor* Christocentric interpretation, the preacher will have either obscured the gospel of Jesus Christ or subverted the nature of Scripture. Both errors are unacceptable. Our hearers need us to preach Christ competently for the sake of their spiritual health. Their understanding of the Bible, of the triune God and His gospel, and of living as a Christian will be shaped for good or ill depending on the soundness of our approach. If the Old Testament is to be preached as Christian Scripture, then let us learn to do it well.

That's what this little book is all about. *Your Old Testament Sermon Needs to Get Saved* is a practical handbook for preaching Christ from the Old Testament. Much of the literature on this topic falls into one of three categories: (1) lengthy academic books, many of which tend more toward theory than practice; (2) general preaching books that offer suggestions for Christ-centered preaching without formulating a comprehensive method; and (3) study books—e.g., commentaries, biblical theologies, Bible study curriculum—whose goal is to provide the fruit of Christ-centered interpretation rather than to explain the root itself.

All these resources are valuable. Many of them are outstanding. However, the need remains for a simple and practical guide for preaching Christ from the Old Testament. That's my aim for this book. What you read in the pages that follow is the Christ-centered approach to the Old Testament that has guided my own preaching and teaching throughout the second decade of my pastoral ministry. It's a comprehensive approach, cobbled together from the best interpretive insights of others. It's a practical application of biblical theology that has enabled me to preach Christ from every part of the Law, the Prophets, and the Writings. My desire is that busy pastors will benefit from what I believe is a sound and straightforward hermeneutic.

Although I'm writing to pastors, the interpretive approach I offer here will be useful to anyone who instructs others from the Old Testament. Welcome, Sunday school teachers and Bible study leaders! As you come across the words "sermon" and "preach" in this book, just transpose them to your specific teaching context, and you'll have little trouble following along.

Several important clarifications need to be made before starting. First, this book isn't about the Old Testament being generically Christ-centered. Rather, the interpretive approach I'm commending arises from a conviction that every jot and tittle of the Old Testament has been fulfilled in Christ. Therefore, it's not only justifiable but essential that we interpret every detail in light of Christ. There are some who disagree. Though they agree that the Old Testament is about Christ, they question the validity of it being so thoroughly Christ-centered. In Part 1, I seek to show why their skepticism is misplaced.

Second, the interpretive approach I'm commending focuses on preaching the *incarnate* Christ, as in, the man named Jesus. Yes, the pre-incarnate Christ may indeed be present in the Old Testament as the eternal Logos, the Angel of the Lord, the Commander of the Lord's army, or the Wisdom of God. But as Sidney Greidanus contends, "All these so-called solutions sidestep the real problem of preaching Christ from the Old Testament. According to the New Testament, preaching Christ is preaching Jesus of Nazareth as the climax of God's revelation of Himself."[2] To preach Christ, biblically speaking, is to preach *Jesus* Christ. Providing a simple hermeneutic for doing so is the goal of Part 2. In other words, Part 2 is the heart of the book.

Third, I'm using the word "Christ" in a loaded sense. "Christ" is technically a title for Jesus, not a name. It refers to Jesus' office as the Anointed One, Messiah, and King. However, as a sort of shorthand, I'm also using "Christ" to refer to the entirety of Jesus' life and work. So when I say "Christ," I mean the Christ, who is Jesus; I mean the Christ, who died on the cross and rose on the third day as a substitutionary sacrifice for sinners; I mean the Christ, in whom God's kingdom is coming on earth. These terms are not identical—"Christ," "Jesus," "gospel," and "kingdom" can each be parsed according to its own specific meaning. But I'm using them interchangeably, and in each one I comprehend the others. So when I speak of preaching Christ from the Old Testament, I'm talking about preaching the Old Testament in light of Jesus and the gospel and the kingdom inaugurated in His coming. If the word "Christ" were a freight train, picture it rumbling down the tracks carrying the heaviest load possible.

In the last section of the book, Part 3, I risk assuming that Parts 1 and 2 have been convincing. You've been persuaded to preach Christ from the Old Testament, and you're eager and equipped to lift up Jesus from every Old Testament passage. Now, be careful! You'll want to avoid several problems that are unique to Christ-centered exposition. But with those cautions in mind, go for it! There are many benefits to enjoy once you begin preaching Jesus from the first two-thirds of the Bible.

May God be pleased to save the lost and strengthen the saved as you preach Christ from the Old Testament. Whether you're preaching from the Law, the Prophets, or the Writings, may the church you serve flourish in Christian maturity. To that end, we need to begin by making certain that our Christ-centered convictions are correct. We need to nail down the necessity of preaching every Old Testament text in light of Jesus and the gospel.

We need to deal with the rock in our shoe.

Part 1

Why Should I Preach Christ from the Old Testament?

1

Exegetical Necessity

Pastor Adam is preaching about the Lord's covenant with David in 2 Samuel 7. He's studied the text carefully. While preaching, he elaborates on the historical and cultural background of David's story in a way that transports his listeners into the moment. He explains David's intent to build a house for the Lord. He creatively imagines what David must have felt when the prophet Nathan returns with a divine "no" from God. He highlights the Lord's amazing promise to David—that instead of David building a house for God, God would build a house for David. Pastor Adam walks the congregation through the entire episode scene-by-scene, highlighting what the text teaches about God and what it teaches about man. Throughout the message, he urges the church to trust in the Lord.

Sounds like an excellent sermon, doesn't it?

Certainly, the sermon is commendable in that it's text-driven, God-centered, and faith-inspiring. But beyond these desirable qualities, we shouldn't call the sermon excellent. At best, the sermon is deficient; at worst, it's a failure. Why? Not because of what Pastor Adam said, but because of what he didn't say. Pastor Adam neglected to interpret and apply the text in light of Jesus. The gospel wasn't present, and the sermon assumed people could relate to the God of 2 Samuel 7 apart from Christ.

Of all Old Testament Scriptures, 2 Samuel 7 seems like especially fertile ground for preaching Christ. It's not as if the connection between the Davidic covenant and Jesus is obscure. If you're familiar with the Bible, you realize how easy it should be to draw a line between the promise made to David and its fulfillment in Christ. But Pastor Adam drew no line. Perhaps he thought the line was so obvious that he didn't *need* to draw it. Maybe you agree.

By the way, this sermon isn't made-up. I heard it myself. I've changed the preacher's name because I believe in the Golden Rule! And I chose the name Adam because the sermon could have been any man's. I've preached many sermons like it myself. So, yes, I have a rock in my hand right now, but it's not for throwing. Rather, like I said in the Introduction, it's for placing in the shoe of all the Pastor Adams out there.

What about you? Do you think it's unnecessary to preach Christ in every sermon, as long as you speak truthfully about the text itself and encourage people to trust in God?

FOR THE UNCONVINCED

The heart of this handbook is practical methodology. I want to help pastors know *how* to preach Christ from the Old Testament. But before we get to the How, we need to begin with the Why. If you're already convinced from Scripture about the necessity of preaching Christ from the text itself, then feel free to skim or even to skip these first two chapters and move on to Parts 2 and 3 of the book. If, however, you're unconvinced—if you believe Pastor Adam's sermon was just fine—then please keep reading.

It's vital to ask *why* you should preach Christ from the Old Testament. You don't just need a method, you need meaning. You don't just need a process, you need purpose. If there's anything your preaching of Christ should be, it should be convictional. The preacher ought to feel as if he *must* exalt Jesus. He should feel, like Peter and John, that he "cannot but speak" of Him (Acts 4:20).

Let me show you how I came to believe this.

THE KEY TO INTERPRETING EVERYTHING

We start with the simple but sweeping confession: *Jesus is Lord*. Take a second to ponder the weight of that three-word sentence. Could there be a more persuasive argument for preaching Christ from the Old Testament? If Jesus is Lord, then He is Lord over the Old Testament—and Lord over our Old Testament sermons, too.

But some preachers haven't recognized the Lordship of Christ over the interpretive process. Consequently, except for preaching Christ from obvious messianic prophecies, they mine the Old Testament mainly for theological truths, spiritual principles, and practical applications. Need a sermon on parenting? Deuteronomy 6 will do. Are you addressing leaders? The kings of Judah and Israel provide some leadership lessons. Is your church in a building project? Nehemiah is your go-to book. Want to preach on finances or communication? Consider Proverbs.

I don't mean to imply that the Old Testament is impractical for Christian living. On the contrary, the Old Testament is inspired by God to equip us for every good work in Christ (2 Tim. 3:15–17). But too many preachers make little or no effort to understand the connection of the text to the person and work of Jesus. The text serves a utilitarian purpose rather than a Christological one.

Simply put, these Old Testament sermons need to get saved.

I got the idea of a sermon getting saved from Graeme Goldsworthy's *Gospel-Centered Hermeneutics*. Let me share two key quotes, and you'll understand what I mean by a sermon getting "saved." In the first quote, Goldsworthy asks us to make the connection between the Bible-as-true and Jesus-as-Lord:

> If the biblical story is true, Christ is the only Saviour for human-kind and there is room for no other way to God. If the story is true, Jesus Christ is the interpretative key to every fact in the universe and, of course, the Bible is one such fact. He is thus the hermeneu-tic principle that applies first to the Bible as the ground for under-standing, and also to the whole of reality. . . . the person and work of Jesus Christ are foundational for evangelical hermeneutics.[1]

Goldsworthy's if/then reasoning is illuminating. *If* the story of the Bible is true, *then* Jesus is the only Savior and the key to interpreting everything in the universe, including the Bible. In other words, you can't interpret the Scriptures correctly (or any part of reality correctly) unless you interpret them in light of the person and work of Jesus Christ. That's what I mean by an Old Testament sermon getting saved. No matter how many true things are said about the text, a sermon is lost until the Lord Jesus Christ stands in the middle of it.

To put it more practically, you should interpret every Old Testa-ment text the same way you interpret everything else in the world. As a Christian, you already ask yourself (I hope) how the truth of Jesus Christ bears on every situation in your life. That's the right question. You know by faith, as Goldsworthy says, that "Jesus Christ is the inter-pretative key to every fact in the universe." So, when preaching from the Old Testament, keep asking that Christocentric question. You must bring Jesus to bear upon the text.

A second quote from Goldsworthy drives home the point: "If Christ truly is our Lord and Saviour, then he is the Lord and Saviour of our hermeneutics."[2] The Lord and Savior of our hermeneutics— isn't that a helpful thought? Homiletical salvation comes through hermeneutical salvation. Once you grasp the Lordship of Christ in relation to the meaning of your preaching text, your sermon can be saved.

THE EXEGETICAL CASE

Of course that *sounds* right. Who would argue with doing everything under the Lordship of Christ? The question is whether the Bible actually leads us to interpret itself in such a Jesus-focused way.

The answer comes by noticing what Jesus says about the Old Testament, and by observing how His apostles handled the Old Testament. When you see their interpretive convictions, you will be compelled to follow them in viewing every Old Testament text through the lens of the gospel. Here's what we learn from Jesus and the apostles.

First, every part of the Old Testament—the Law, the Prophets, and the Writings—points to Jesus. Many of these pointers to Jesus are obvious: promises that lead to Jesus, prophecies that speak of Jesus, patterns that foreshadow the work of Jesus. Every part of the Old Testament contains some of these obvious pointers.

The Gospel of Luke records two of Jesus' most familiar statements about Old Testament interpretation. The first statement occurs during Jesus' encounter with two men on the road to Emmaus. A pair of disciples plods along, discussing the sad events surrounding Jesus' crucifixion and the bewildering report of an empty tomb. In the middle of their conversation, a stranger draws close. The stranger, of course, is Jesus, but His identity is hidden from them. Upon hearing their disappointment and confusion, Jesus rebukes them for their hesitancy to believe the prophets.

Luke records Jesus' words: "O foolish ones, and slow of heart to believe all that the prophets have spoken! Was it not necessary that the Christ should suffer these things and enter into his glory?" (24:25–26). Luke then adds this key sentence: "And beginning with Moses and all the Prophets, [Jesus] interpreted to them in all the Scriptures the things concerning himself" (v. 27). *Moses and the prophets. All the Scriptures.* On the Emmaus road, Jesus used the whole Old Testament to explain Himself to the disciples. Hold that thought while we add another one to it.

The second relevant statement occurs later that night among a larger group of disciples. Luke includes more detail on this occasion, but we can see the similarity between these words and Jesus' words on the Emmaus road:

> Then he said to them, "These are my words that I spoke to you while I was still with you, that everything written about me in the Law of Moses and the Prophets and the Psalms must be fulfilled." Then he opened their minds to understand the Scriptures, and said to them, "Thus it is written, that the Christ should suffer and on the third day rise from the dead, and that repentance and forgiveness of sins should be proclaimed in his name to all nations, beginning from Jerusalem." (Luke 24:44–47)

Jesus' reference to "the Law of Moses and the Prophets and the Psalms" corresponds to the three major sections of the Hebrew Bible: the Law, the Prophets, and the Writings.[3] Here Jesus is reiterating what He said earlier that day: the entire Old Testament speaks of Him.

Jesus' two statements clarify what a Christ-centered hermeneutic for the Old Testament should entail—and it's much more specific than we might have guessed. To preach Christ from the Old Testament is not to preach a *fuzzy* Christ, offering vague hints about His future work or speculating about His pre-incarnate presence in one story or another. Rather, we learn that the Law, the Prophets, and the Writings outline the contours of the Messiah's earthly ministry. The disciples should have read these Scriptures in a way that prepared them for the cross, the empty tomb, for repentance and forgiveness of sins in Jesus' name, and for the inclusion of the nations in His salvation (vv. 26, 46–47; cf. "in accordance with the Scriptures" in 1 Cor.

15:3–4). That's pretty specific! In short, to preach Christ from the Old Testament is to proclaim nothing less than the gospel of Jesus Christ.

To summarize, Luke 24 lays the foundation for interpreting all three parts of the Old Testament in light of Jesus. The Law, the Prophets, and the Writings point to the incarnate Christ's life, death, resurrection, and ministry to the nations. Jesus interprets the Scriptures this way, rebukes those who don't, and illuminates His disciples so that they can.

As preachers, are we seeing what Jesus means for us to see?

This first exegetical point is easy to accept in reference to *obvious* messianic texts, such as the promise to Abraham, the typology of the Passover lamb, or the Suffering Servant prophecy. But what about when there's no obvious pointer to Jesus in the text? Is it necessary to interpret less obvious texts in light of Christ?

Second, Old Testament texts that don't contain explicit anticipation of Jesus are part of an Old Testament canon that by its very nature witnesses to Jesus. This point is vital for us to settle in our minds. In preaching Christ from the Old Testament, we should feel compelled to relate *every* text to Jesus, not just the texts that are obviously about Him.

John 5 is instructive in this regard. Jesus has been accused of making Himself equal with God, and so His opponents desire to kill Him (v. 18). In response, Jesus summons multiple witnesses to testify to His identity (cf. Deut. 19:15). The witnesses, according to John 5:30–47, include John the Baptist, Jesus' own works, God the Father, the Scriptures, and Moses. For our purposes, the witness of the Scriptures is paramount.

Jesus calls on the Scriptures—what we call the Old Testament— to serve as a witness to His identity. He charges His opponents with failing to perceive the Christocentric witness of the Old Testament: "You search the Scriptures because you think that in them you have eternal life; and it is they that bear witness about me, yet you refuse to come to me that you may have life" (John 5:39–40). The failure of Jesus' opponents was not due to slackness. His opponents were in fact diligent students of the Old Testament. Yet for all their expertise and energy, they failed to grasp the very nature of Scripture as a witness to the incarnate Christ. God never intended the Old Testament by itself to give life. Rather, it was from the beginning a signpost pointing to Jesus Christ. Eternal life, Jesus says, is not found *in* the Scriptures but *through* the Scriptures as they bear witness about Him.

Jesus' language here about the nature of the Scriptures suggests that He has in view more than obvious messianic texts.[4] He seems to be saying that the Old Testament is pervasively Christ-centered, that its very fabric has been woven with Him in mind. Which means, like thread running through a piece of fabric, the entirety of the Scriptures relates to Jesus.[5]

Jesus' assertion forces us to an inescapable conclusion: to understand the Old Testament in a way that marginalizes Jesus or neglects Him altogether is to understand the Scriptures wrongly. According to Jesus, failing to understand the Old Testament this way is not merely wrong but damning. The faulty hermeneutic of Jesus' opponents has robbed them, Jesus says, of nothing less than salvation (John 5:34). They do not have eternal life (v. 40). Despite all their searching, despite all their educated and earnest Bible study, Jesus' opponents had totally missed the point of the Scriptures by failing to see how they witness to Him.

> **To understand the Old Testament in a way that marginalizes Jesus or neglects Him altogether is to understand the Scriptures wrongly.**

The failure to employ a Christ-centered hermeneutic to the Old

Testament is spiritually deadly. We either understand the Old Testament in a way that leads to Jesus and to eternal life in Him, or we misunderstand the Old Testament in a way that brings Jesus' rebuke down upon our own heads. God inspired the Scriptures to lead us and our hearers to Christ. As preachers, we must preach them that way.

Third, no Old Testament text can be rightly interpreted without understanding how it has been fulfilled in Jesus. Another relevant and well-known passage linking Christ and the Old Testament is found in the Gospel of Matthew. In the Sermon on the Mount, Jesus says,

> Do not think that I have come to abolish the Law or the Prophets; I have not come to abolish them but to fulfill them. For truly, I say to you, until heaven and earth pass away, not an iota, not a dot, will pass from the Law until all is accomplished. Therefore whoever relaxes one of the least of these commandments and teaches others to do the same will be called least in the kingdom of heaven, but whoever does them and teaches them will be called great in the kingdom of heaven. For I tell you, unless your righteousness exceeds that of the scribes and Pharisees, you will never enter the kingdom of heaven. (Matt. 5:17–20)

Several key observations must be made about this text. To begin with, Jesus is talking about the Old Testament. Jesus' references to the Law and the Prophets (v. 17), and then only to the Law (v. 18), are commonly understood to include the entirety of the Hebrew Scriptures.[6]

Next, Jesus unambiguously affirms the abiding validity of the Old Testament. His ministry is not one of abolition (v. 17). All Scripture endures, even the tiniest strokes of the pen, until heaven and earth pass away (v. 18). Because attention to the commands of Scripture divides the least from the greatest in the kingdom (v. 19), no responsible Christian can set aside the Old Testament as irrelevant. And yet, we must not read the Old Testament as if Jesus hasn't come, as if the Old Testament were purely Jewish history and not a Christian book.

That leads to our final and most vital observation: Jesus drives an interpretive stake in the ground in asserting that all the Old Testament is fulfilled in Him. In other words, Jesus changes how we read the Old Testament. Not just *parts* of the Old Testament, but *all* of it is fulfilled in Him! Every dot and every iota of every passage—every jot and tittle, as the King James famously put it—is fulfilled in the life and teaching of the incarnate Christ.[7] Jesus' fulfillment language here clearly goes beyond obvious messianic promises and prophecies and patterns. It includes everything!

It would be difficult to overstate the hermeneutical significance of this. Jesus is the goal of every detail in the Bible. Which means no Old Testament text can be rightly understood without grasping its fulfillment in Him. Every passage, without exception, requires an interpretation involving Jesus. New Testament scholar Craig Blomberg boils it down:

[Jesus'] claim has massive hermeneutical implications and challenges both classic Reformed and Dispensationalist perspectives. It is inadequate to say either that none of the Old Testament applies unless it is explicitly reaffirmed in the New or that all the Old Testament applies unless it is explicitly revoked in the New. Rather, all the Old Testament remains normative and relevant for Jesus' followers (2 Tim 3:16), but none of it can rightly be interpreted until one understands how it has been fulfilled in Christ. Every Old Testament text must be viewed in light of Jesus' person and ministry and the changes introduced by the new covenant he inaugurated.[8]

In Matthew 5:17–20, Jesus tells us the Old Testament Scriptures are here to stay. But they must be understood in light of His life and teaching. Here, Jesus not only validates but necessitates a Christocentric approach to every text of the Old Testament.

Fourth, having been taught by Jesus how to read the Bible, the apostles adopted a broad prophetic understanding of the Old Testament. To observe that Jesus' apostles preached Christ from the Old Testament requires about as much insight as a child picking out his mother in a roomful of women. The Old Testament was *the* text for apostolic witness to Christ. In a passage worth quoting at length, Walter Kaiser observes,

> As early as the day of Pentecost (Acts 2:16–36), the apostle Peter used the Old Testament to demonstrate that Jesus' death, burial, and resurrection had been clearly anticipated by the writers of the Old Testament. Peter appealed to the prophet Joel (Joel 2:28–31), to the psalmist (Ps. 16), and to King David's understanding (2 Sam. 7; Ps. 110) to make these same points prior to the appearance of any New Testament literature. A few days later, as Peter and John were going into the temple, he healed a lame man at the temple gate (Acts 3). This occasioned another sermon from Peter, in which he again made direct references to Abraham, Isaac, and Jacob, noting how they pointed "to what [God] had foretold through all the prophets" (Acts 3:18), namely, that Christ must suffer. . . . This pattern of appealing to the Old Testament to demonstrate that Christ is the Messiah was repeated in Stephen's speech in Acts 7 and in Paul's speech in the synagogue at Antioch (Acts 13). . . . The apostles' appeal was directly and solely to the earlier and prior text of the Old Testament itself.[9]

Many other examples could be added to Kaiser's survey, such as Paul using the Scriptures to explain and prove that Jesus is the Christ (Acts 17:1–3); or the Bereans examining the Scriptures daily to verify the truthfulness of the apostolic witness to Jesus (17:11); or Apollos "showing by the Scriptures that the Christ was Jesus" (18:28). Indeed, Paul would later provide a succinct description of apostolic preaching:

"Him we proclaim" (Col. 1:28). The apostles proclaimed Christ, and the text they used to do so was the Old Testament.

Some rabbinic calculations tally 456 Old Testament prophecies of the Messiah or messianic times (this is likely an overestimation).[10] The apostles employed many of these prophetic texts in their proclamation of Jesus as the Christ. Modern Christian interpreters readily embrace such an approach to preaching Christ from the Old Testament. And so we're in good company when we recognize the prophetic testimony of the Scriptures to Christ (Matt. 26:56; Rom. 1:1–3; 16:25–26; 2 Cor. 1:20; 1 Peter 1:10–12).

What is somewhat startling, however, is the broadness of the prophetic lens through which the apostles read the Old Testament. Matthew provides the classic example in his interpretation of Jesus' flight to Egypt while in the care of Joseph and Mary (Matt. 2:13–15). Matthew says that the flight and subsequent return was in fulfillment of Hosea's prophecy: "Out of Egypt I called my son" (v. 15). But when we read Hosea's own words, it's not at all apparent that Hosea is prophesying. Hosea 11:1 appears simply to be a historical reference to the Exodus: "When Israel was a child, I loved him, and out of Egypt I called my son."

We ought not be so uncharitable as to suggest that Matthew has misunderstood or misused the Old Testament. There's sound justification for using a prophetic lens that's wide enough to see in Israel the shape of Christ. I will offer justification for this in the next chapter, but for now don't miss the basic point: the fulfillment of the Old Testament isn't limited to predictive messianic prophecies. Rather, in some legitimate sense, the entire Old Testament embodies messianic promise. The whole text leans forward toward Christ.

Once we grasp this truth, Matthew's link between Israel and Jesus—between Hosea's "prophecy" and its "fulfillment" in Jesus' return from Egypt—becomes less fantastical and more intelligible. Of course, one is left wondering how this broader understanding of prophetic fulfillment can be accurately explained, but the fact remains that

Christ can be proclaimed from Old Testament texts in a manner that pushes the boundaries of our own prophetic understanding. Matthew wasn't mistaken.

Fifth, the apostles encouraged reading the entire Old Testament as Christian Scripture. The previous observation is an example of how Matthew read the Old Testament with a broad prophetic understanding of fulfillment in Christ. The present observation is that Paul intends for us to read the Old Testament in the same way.

My experience with a well-known passage about the Old Testament, 2 Timothy 3:15–17, is that people speed through the first part on the way to the last part. But notice carefully the entirety of what Paul tells Timothy. The "sacred writings," he says—what we call the Old Testament:

> Are able to make you wise for salvation through faith in Christ Jesus. All Scripture is breathed out by God and profitable for teaching, for reproof, for correction, and for training in righteousness, that the man of God may be complete, equipped for every good work. (2 Tim. 3:15–17)

All these verses go together. In fact, the redemptive focus of the first sentence *controls* the comprehensive scope of the second sentence. To be just a tad provocative, Paul isn't saying that all Scripture is profitable for making us competent *Jews*. He's saying that all Scripture is profitable for making us competent *Christians*. And we don't have to infer that this is what Paul means—he states it plainly. The sacred writings, he says, are able to make us wise for salvation through faith in Christ Jesus.

Paul's point couldn't be clearer, and the implication of his point must not be missed. The book that we call the Old Testament isn't merely Jewish Scripture. It's Christian Scripture. Every Old Testament text is profitable because it serves in some way to make God's people wise for salvation through faith in Christ Jesus. That is, it teaches, reproves, corrects, and trains us in righteousness *as Christians*; it completes us *as Christians*; it equips us for every good work *as Christians*. Paul is commending the Old Testament to us as Christian Scripture. The preacher, therefore, in order to preach the Scriptures accurately, must grapple with how every Old Testament text relates to Jesus.

A STRONG CORD

If we weave together each strand of this exegetical argument, then preaching Jesus Christ from every passage in the Old Testament becomes a cord not easily broken. The entire Old Testament—the Law, the Prophets, and the Writings—contains promises or prophecies or patterns about Christ. Furthermore, the texts that don't contain obvious promises and prophesies and patterns are still part of an Old Testament canon that by its very nature witnesses to Christ. Therefore, as Jesus Himself teaches, no Old Testament text can be interpreted rightly without understanding how it has been fulfilled in Him. The apostles, having learned from Jesus how to read the Scriptures like this, adopted a broad prophetic understanding of the Old Testament and encouraged the saints to read the Old Testament as Christian Scripture.

I hope you feel the force of this argument. You don't have to rely exclusively on the New Testament to preach about Jesus and the gospel and salvation and discipleship. The whole Bible is at your disposal. So start exalting Christ and teaching people how to walk with Him—*in every passage you preach*. You need only to understand how to do it.

But before we get to the How, we must add to the Why. There's more to be said about the necessity of your Old Testament sermon getting saved.

2

Theological Necessity

Nineteenth century Danish author Hans Christian Anderson wrote the short story "The Emperor's New Clothes." I'm sure you've heard of it. It's about an emperor with an obsessive love for clothes, and two enterprising thieves who sell him a "magical" outfit that can be seen only by intelligent people. The emperor parades through the streets in his expensive new suit that doesn't actually exist—and an entire kingdom, from emperor to peasant, is too proud to admit they can't see the suit. The story ends with a little child crying out, "But the emperor has no clothes!"

Is that what's going on here? Am I encouraging you to see things in the Bible that aren't really there? Perhaps a Christ-centered hermeneutic has no clothes.

That's what some people believe. "Jesus isn't present in every passage," they say, "and you ought not pretend that He is. Don't read Christ into the text when He's not there."

What do you think? Do you believe there are portions of the Old Testament that have nothing to do with Jesus? When your passage doesn't contain an obvious messianic connection, have you been content to leave Christ out of your sermon?

Perhaps you wouldn't go that far. Maybe you *do* feel the need to preach Christ, even when you don't see the connection. And so you append the gospel to your sermon as part of a closing appeal. That was my practice for many years. Though it's better to append Christ to a sermon than leave Him out altogether, you must consider whether the Father means for His Son to be preached as an appendix to the sermon rather than as the heart. Until the conclusion, such sermons are suitable for the synagogue.

Hopefully, you'll never preach another synagogue sermon. If exegesis hasn't persuaded you to preach Christ from every Old Testament passage, maybe theology will! What follows are five vital points of theology that should compel you to place Christ at the heart of every Old Testament sermon.[1]

PROGRESSIVE REVELATION

That God reveals Himself progressively throughout history is widely accepted among scholars. Edmund Clowney writes,

> The Bible records revelation given in the course of history. This revelation was not given at one point, nor in the form of a theological dictionary. It was given progressively, for the process of revelation accompanies the process of redemption.[2]

Let's not be confused about what this means. Progressive revelation doesn't mean that earlier revelation is inferior to later revelation, or that later revelation makes earlier revelation obsolete. Rather, it means that later revelation builds on earlier revelation. Later revelation clarifies, refines, and fulfills earlier revelation.

Preaching Christ from the Old Testament depends on progressive revelation. Imagine if the two testaments were disjointed, telling two disconnected stories. Or imagine if the New Testament *invalidated* the Old Testament. If either case were true, there'd be no basis for preaching

Christ from the Old Testament. But thankfully, the opposite is true! The Old and New Testaments are organically connected through the unfolding revelation of God. Thus, preaching Christ from the Old Testament is not only possible but sensible and even obligatory.

The opening sentence of Hebrews attests to Scripture's progressive revelation: "Long ago, at many times and in many ways, God spoke to our fathers by the prophets, but in these last days he has spoken to us by his Son, whom he appointed the heir of all things, through whom he also created the world" (Heb. 1:1–2). When composers want a musician to increase volume, they place a symbol in the music called a *crescendo*. In Scripture, the volume swells throughout the prophets, reaching the height of its crescendo in the life, death, and resurrection of Jesus Christ.

I love how William Lane captures this. Commenting on Hebrews 1:1–2, Lane writes of Jesus as the Son:

> Through whom God spoke his final and decisive word. . . . God's continuing disclosure of himself found its ultimate expression in the revelation through the Son. . . . The OT witness actually foreshadowed the utterance of God's decisive and climactic word. . . . The ministry of the prophets marked the preparatory phase of that history. . . . What God said through the Son clarified the intention of the word spoken to the fathers. From this perspective, the recent revelation in the Son is viewed as fulfillment.[3]

What a glorious cascade of adjectives! Jesus is the final, decisive, and climactic word that God has spoken. He's the ultimate expression of revelation. He's the Son for whom the prophets prepared and in whom God clarified the patriarchal promises. He's the fulfillment of the entire stream of redemptive history.

The theological implication here is big. If Christ is the final word from God, then all previous words lead to Him. To preach those

> **Jesus is the final, decisive, and climactic word that God has spoken. He's the fulfillment of the entire stream of redemptive history.**

previous words—those Old Testament words—without tracing them to their fulfillment is to preach an unfinished story. The Old Testament isn't complete in itself. Rather, it's designed by God to end as a nail-biting cliffhanger, and the New Testament is the tension-relieving conclusion.

Let's do a little exercise. Answer the following question after filling in the blank with the topics below:

How is/are _____ fulfilled in Christ?

- the patriarchal promises
- the covenant of circumcision
- the exodus
- the tabernacle
- the sacrificial system
- the holiness code
- kingship
- prophecy
- wisdom

To explain a patriarchal promise or the covenant of circumcision; to exult in God's redemption in the exodus or the creation of the tabernacle; to understand the food laws or the sacrificial system; to expound on the succession of kings or the prophetic pronouncements; to extol the need for wisdom—to preach on *any* of these topics without explaining how Christ fulfills them is to tell the congregation only part of the story. It's like turning off a movie right before the climax. Don't do it!

No Old Testament text is the final word because Jesus Christ is the final word. The truth of progressive revelation must lead the preacher to preach every Old Testament text in light of the final word that God has spoken.

THE NEW COVENANT IN CHRIST

Even stronger theological warrant for preaching Christ from the Old Testament resides in God's establishment of a new covenant. Every preacher must grasp the significance of what God is doing through the covenants. Miss this, and every sermon will be skewed. The Old Testament simply cannot be preached correctly without interpreting it in light of the new covenant. Let me justify this claim by answering four questions.

First, what is a covenant? To put it simply, a covenant is a relational agreement, detailing how two parties will relate to each other. Typically, the agreement involves obligations between one or both parties. In the Old Testament, we see God graciously initiating covenants with Adam, Noah, Abraham, Israel, and David. Other covenants are depicted, but these covenants stand out as having significant redemptive significance.

Second, how are the major covenants in the Bible related? If redemptive history were a river, the covenants are the riverbanks. God's redemptive work flows throughout history along a covenantal channel. To put it another way, the covenants form the plot structure of the entire biblical story. They are, as Peter Gentry and Stephen Wellum put it, "the backbone of the biblical narrative."[4]

Third, what story unfolds in and around and through God's covenants? The covenantal story is the story of God's kingdom on earth. It begins with the goodness of creation, over which Adam and

Eve are placed to rule as vice-regents of God. Tragically, however, Adam and Eve sin against God, bringing God's curse upon the world. Nevertheless, God graciously promises to destroy evil and redeem the fallen cosmos. God will send a new ruler into the world through the offspring of woman.

THE RIVERBANKS OF REDEMPTIVE HISTORY	
THE MAJOR COVENANTS	**MAIN SCRIPTURES**
The Covenant with Adam	Genesis 1–3 (cf. Hosea 6:7)
The Covenant with Noah	Genesis 6–9
The Covenant with Abraham	Genesis 12, 15, 17
The Covenant with Israel	Exodus 19:3b–8
The Covenant with David	2 Samuel 7; Psalm 89
The New Covenant	Jeremiah 31–34; Ezekiel 34–39

The rest of the story flows out of this initial promise of redemption. In His covenant with Noah, God promises not to destroy the earth, creating a stable environment for God to keep His redemptive promise. God then initiates a covenant with Abraham in which He promises to create a people for Himself, give them a place to live under His rule, and through them to bless all the nations of the world. God fulfills these promises in the rise of Israel and, later, her redemption from Egyptian slavery. At Sinai, God's people are formally constituted in God's covenant with Israel, and the promise of dwelling in a land under God's blessing is renewed with the stipulation that Israel must live faithfully under God's rule. God then makes a covenant with King David to put a ruler on His throne forever. And finally, due to Israel's covenantal unfaithfulness, God graciously promises to establish a new covenant in which God's people are forgiven of sin and given hearts to honor God.

The climax of the covenantal story—the fulfillment of all God's promises—arrives not in the Old Testament but in the New. During a Passover meal in an upper room, Luke tells us:

[Jesus] took bread, and when he had given thanks, he broke it and gave it to them, saying, "This is my body, which is given for you. Do this in remembrance of me." And likewise the cup after they had eaten, saying, "This cup that is poured out for you is the new covenant in my blood." (Luke 22:19–20)

In Christ, the new covenant has finally arrived! Jesus is the promised seed of woman, the offspring of Abraham, the true Israel, the Son of David, the one through whom our hearts are made new. In short, Jesus is the promised Redeemer King that the Old Testament taught us to anticipate. Via His life, death, resurrection, and ascension, all the promises of God find their Yes in Him. And so we utter our Amen to God for His glory (2 Cor. 1:20). The long-awaited kingdom has dawned in Christ.

Fourth, what bearing does the new covenant have on Old Testament preaching? I hope the answer is obvious. The preacher must not disregard the fulfillment of God's kingdom in the new covenant. To preach from the Old Testament as if the new covenant hasn't been inaugurated is to make a serious hermeneutical error. There's no covenantal epoch—there's no text of the Old Testament—that hasn't given way to the reality of our new covenant relationship with God through His

Son. There simply is no other way of relating to God except through the new covenant. Therefore, the only way we can accurately interpret the Old Testament is to read it in light of its fulfillment.

The author of Hebrews states that "in speaking of a new covenant, [God] makes the first one obsolete. And what is becoming obsolete and growing old is ready to vanish away" (Heb. 8:13). We must be careful to distinguish between the Old Testament as a whole and God's old covenant with Israel. To say that the old covenant is obsolete doesn't mean that the Old Testament is obsolete (Matt. 5:17–20; 2 Tim. 3:15–17). Rather, the point of Hebrews is that the new covenant in Christ has rendered the *old covenant* obsolete. God's covenant with Israel is no longer useful; it's beyond its time.[5]

Any preacher, then, who preaches from the Old Testament as if the old covenant is still an operable system of relating to God makes a fatal interpretive mistake. To be sure, the Old Testament Law stipulates Israel's old covenant obedience; the Old Testament Prophets commend or condemn Israel based on their faithfulness to that Law; and the Old Testament Writings explore faith and wisdom in the context of the old covenant. *Yet the old covenant is now obsolete.*

According to the apostle Paul, the only hope anyone has for accurately interpreting the old covenant is by reading it in light of the new. Contrasting believers with unbelieving Israel, Paul writes,

Since we have such a hope, we are very bold, not like Moses, who would put a veil over his face so that the Israelites might not gaze at the outcome of what was being brought to an end. But their minds were hardened. For to this day, when they read the old covenant, that same veil remains unlifted, because only through Christ is it taken away. Yes, to this day whenever Moses is read a veil lies over their hearts. But when one turns to the Lord, the veil is removed. (2 Cor. 3:12–16)

Unbelieving Israel, because they haven't turned to Christ in faith, cannot see how the glory of the gospel shines back upon the old covenant. Israel remains blind to the old covenant's witness to Jesus. Believers, on the other hand, once were blind but now they see. They peer into the old covenant with uplifted veils and perceive its witness to Jesus. Paul couldn't be clearer: only in Christ and His new covenant is the old covenant understood.

The new covenant provides persuasive theological warrant for holding up every facet of the Old Testament to the light of Jesus and His gospel. As someone once said, "The shining of the moon can be understood only in terms of the shining of the sun."[6] Preaching from the Old Testament without perceiving its illumination by the New is to preach in the dark.

CANONICAL CONTEXT

I once taught a seminar titled "Faithful to the Text, Unfaithful to Jesus." Do you realize that you can earnestly desire to be faithful to a biblical text, study it carefully, preach or teach it powerfully, and still be unfaithful to Jesus?

How is that possible? The answer is simple: you're unfaithful to Jesus when you disregard the context of the Old Testament. And context isn't found simply in the paragraphs before and after a text. Nor is it exhausted by a whole book or even the scope of the Old Testament. Those aspects are crucial, of course, but if that's where you stop, then your contextual boundaries are too narrow. When you think of the context of a text, you need to think about the entire Bible.

You've heard the saying, "No man is an island." It's from a poem by John Donne:

> No man is an island entire of itself;
> every man is a piece of the continent,
> a part of the main

With just a little tweaking of these lines, we've got a true statement about every biblical text:

> *No text is an island entire of itself;*
> *every text is a piece of the continent,*
> *a part of the main*

The continent of context is the canon of Scripture. The boundary markers for your text are set in Genesis 1 and Revelation 22.

Genesis through Revelation tells the story of redemptive history. It's the story of God's kingdom through covenant (as seen above)—or, more broadly, the grand story of creation, fall, redemption, and new creation. The story's main character is the incarnate Son of God who heroically substitutes Himself in death for sinners and triumphantly rises from the dead for their salvation. Jesus' resurrection brings life to all who believe, and functions as the first decisive step toward a new heavens and new earth. So preeminent is Christ in His person and work that God will not rest until the entire cosmos is united in Him (Eph. 1:10).

Once you understand these boundaries, you see how a preacher might pursue textual faithfulness yet end up with Christological unfaithfulness. If you understand your text as an island rather than part of a continent—if you understand the text in isolation from the canonical story of redemption in Christ—then no matter how many true things you say about it, you'll end up being unfaithful to Jesus.

A number of years ago I heard a sermon on Isaiah 40—the famous "comfort, comfort my people" passage. The preacher talked eloquently about preparing the way for the Lord, about being a herald of good news, about the Lord tending His flock like a shepherd—all right there in the text. But never once did he talk about the text's fulfillment in Jesus. He made no attempt to connect its obvious gospel foreshadowing to the ministry of Christ. Consequently, his sermon was a masterful and moving exposition in which many true things were said, just not enough true things.

If you want more examples of unfaithful Old Testament sermons, come to my study and look through my files. I'm guilty! I've always been committed to exposition, but I've not always understood context the way I should. As I've come to understand the canonical context of redemption, focused in the person and work of Jesus Christ, my preaching has changed. I've become more rooted in the gospel. I hope you will, too.

The Bible contains sixty-six books, but it's one book, inspired by one author, telling one grand story of salvation. The unity of Scripture makes canonical interpretation not only viable but essential. Just as we seek to understand a chapter in a novel, or a scene in a movie, or an act in a play, so we must interpret each passage in light of the entire Bible. The canon is our context.

CHRIST, OUR MEDIATOR

So much exegetical and theological argumentation comes down to this: Jesus Christ is the one mediator between God and men (1 Tim. 2:5). If this truth doesn't upset our synagogue sermons, nothing will. In establishing a comprehensive Christ-centered approach to the Old Testament, the mediatory role of Jesus cannot be overemphasized. It demands that we reckon with Him in every aspect of our relationship with God, including how we learn to relate to Him from the Old Testament.

Nail this down: you'll never preach to one person who can have fellowship with God apart from Jesus. There's no scriptural example they can follow, no command they can obey, no warning they can heed, no repentance they can offer, no praise they can give the Father—except through Christ.

The New Testament frequently portrays Jesus in terms of exclusive mediation. Jesus likened Himself to "the door" through which His sheep find pasture with God (John 10:9). He is "the way, and the truth, and the life," apart from whom no one can come to the Father (14:6). The Father cannot even be known apart from the Son (Matt. 11:27), nor is there salvation in any other name (Acts 4:12). To "have" Jesus is to possess life; not to have Him is death (1 John 5:12). All obedience is to be rendered to God through faith in Christ (Rom. 1:5).

Texts like these make it negligent and unloving for preachers to exclude Christ from a sermon. Why would we want to preach any text without relating it to Christ? What would embolden us to neglect the mediator in whom all Scripture is fulfilled and through whom every response to Scripture must pass? How could we presume that a Christless sermon would be a safe sermon for anyone to hear?

The mediatory role of Christ Jesus demands a Christ-centered exposition of every Scripture.

THE *TELOS* OF PREACHING

One final theological consideration must be made when determining whether every Old Testament text must be related to Christ: the *telos* of preaching. *Telos* is the Greek word for "end" or "goal." What's the *telos* of preaching? What's the desired end or goal in our proclamation of Scripture?

The way a preacher answers these questions profoundly impacts his preaching. If you believe the *telos* of preaching is to produce good people, your sermons will likely emphasize behavior and morality. If you believe the *telos* is knowledge, your messages may tend to be academic and impractical. If the *telos* is a happy congregation, your sermons will probably be light and entertaining. If the *telos* is repentance, heaviness and conviction will be expected.

Every sermon is governed by the preacher's understanding of preaching—regardless of the text. So, what is the *telos* of Christian preaching?

Thankfully, the New Testament supplies the wisdom we need to answer this question. Ephesians clarifies the divinely appointed purpose of pastors and teachers. They are "to equip the saints for the work of ministry, for building up the body of Christ, until we all attain to the unity of the faith and of the knowledge of the Son of God, to mature manhood, to the measure of the stature of the fullness of Christ" (4:12–13). If God desires pastoring and teaching to result in the congregation becoming mature in Christ, then every sermon should aim in that direction.

Colossians offers a more compact statement of the *telos* of preaching: "Him we proclaim, warning everyone and teaching everyone with all wisdom, that we may present everyone mature in Christ" (1:28). Again, we see that the divinely appointed end of preaching is maturity in Christ. And maturity in Christ doesn't come through sermons that tack on Christ at the end, or leave Him out altogether. Instead, maturity in Christ comes through the proclamation of Christ. The pronoun placement is emphatic—"*Him* we proclaim"—suggesting that Christ should have a prominent position in the sermon. In order for people to be presented mature in Christ, Christ must be presented to them.

Does honoring Christ as the *telos* of preaching limit the preacher to obvious messianic texts? No, it spurs on the preacher to discern the ways in which every text relates to Christ. Whether you're preaching from the Law, the Prophets, or the Writings—whether you're preaching narrative or poetry or law—whether you're dealing with ethical concerns or biographical illustrations—the *telos* of your sermon ought to be Christ.

Do you want to see people formed into the image of Christ? Then let Christ stand at the heart of all your Old Testament sermons.

CUMULATIVE FORCE

A nail must be hit multiple times before it sinks into a piece of wood. One or two blows won't do it. In this chapter, our hammer has hit the Christ-centered nail on the head five times. Have the blows been successful? Consider what theology has taught us:

1. God's revelation of redemption unfolds progressively throughout Scripture, climaxing in the person and work of Jesus Christ, who is Himself the final word from God.
2. The old covenant can no longer be understood properly unless read in light of the new.
3. The entire canon of Scripture forms the outer contextual boundary for every preaching text.
4. Jesus is the exclusive mediator between God and men, the one in whom all Scripture is fulfilled and through whom all obedience to God is rendered.
5. The *telos* of preaching is nothing less than the church's maturity in Jesus Christ.

These theological truths demand that we preach Christ from every Old Testament text. Christ *must* be preached! Whatever text the preacher takes up, let him take it all the way up into Christ.[7]

Part 2

How Do I Preach Christ from the Old Testament?

3

The Preaching Text

Bedford Clapperton Pim, a British naval officer and recognized authority on Central America, wrote of the Panama Railroad,

> I have seen the greatest engineering works of the day . . . but I must confess that when passing backwards and forwards on the Panama Railway, standing on the engine to obtain a good view, I have never been more struck than with the evidence, apparent on every side, of the wonderful skill, endurance, and perseverance, which must have been exercised in its construction.[1]

The Panama Railroad, begun in 1850 and completed in 1855, was the first ocean-to-ocean railroad. The marvel of this engineering feat in a day when no rail had been laid west of the Mississippi is compounded when one realizes that the Panama Railroad had to be cut through a rainforest.

Author David McCullough reminds us of mid-nineteenth century realities that made the railroad survey alone almost inconceivable: no aerial photography, no modern medicines, no insect repellent, no bulldozers, no chain saws, no canned goods, and not one reliable map. No wonder that "mile for mile [the Panama Railroad] appears to have cost more in dollars and human life than any railroad ever built."[2]

In other words, Officer Pim was right to marvel. Connecting the Atlantic and Pacific by rail required a level of skill and perseverance that was nothing short of remarkable.

Connecting the Old Testament to Jesus Christ demands nothing less. Laying the rail between text and fulfillment requires interpretive skill and perseverance because the path isn't always plain. It's one thing to *believe* everything is fulfilled in Christ, but it's another thing entirely to clear a path between the passage and Jesus.

How can Jesus become the Lord and Savior of our hermeneutics? How can our Old Testament sermons get saved?

Even after becoming convinced I needed to preach every Old Testament text in light of Jesus, these questions stumped me. I wasn't sure how to do it without getting kooky. By kooky, I mean finding Jesus in every tent peg of the tabernacle or up in the branches of every terebinth tree in Canaan. Surely becoming a Christ-centered preacher doesn't require standing over the Old Testament like a magician—only, instead of pulling a rabbit out of a hat, we pull Jesus out of the text. We do a little hermeneutical hocus-pocus and—*poof!*—there's Jesus! And the congregation gasps in wonder at our amazing interpretive powers.

Over the years, this fear of hermeneutical magic has been allayed. We don't need magic to preach Christ from the Old Testament. If our exegetical and theological insights are valid (see Part 1), then there's a legitimate way to interpret every text in light of Christ. We just need to be familiar with the ways that Jesus fulfills the Old Testament.

EASY AS 1-2-3 . . . KIND OF

You are now in the heart of this book. Part 2 is the core, the meat and potatoes, the nitty gritty. Here I offer three steps for interpreting every Old Testament text in light of Christ. Together, these steps comprise a simple, practical, and comprehensive method of interpretation, one that I use every time I open the Old Testament—whether preparing to preach or teach, or simply reading the Bible devotionally. By working carefully through the steps, relying on the Holy Spirit's help, you end up with a legitimate Christ-centered understanding of the text. And you'll be ready to exalt Christ in your sermon!

I call the three steps: TEXT, CHRIST, US. Groundbreaking, I know! But it's the direction we want to move—from the Old Testament text, to its fulfillment in Christ, and into our lives through application.

This chapter explains the first step, TEXT. This step is the most familiar of the three, and most conscientious pastors already attempt it. Nonetheless, I hope this chapter will be beneficial.

STEP ONE: TEXT

Step One involves the selection and exegesis of a text for preaching or teaching. My comments on this step will be succinct because most pastors who would pick up a book like this one are already familiar with the exegetical process. There's a preponderance of excellent material on the topic, and my aim isn't to add another book to the pile. Still, I'd like to highlight a few important points regarding the selection and exegesis of a text.

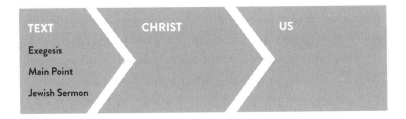

TEXT
Exegesis
Main Point
Jewish Sermon

CHRIST

US

Select a Legitimate Preaching Text

When it comes to Scripture, is there an illegitimate preaching text? In one sense, no. "All Scripture is breathed out by God and profitable" (2 Tim. 3:16). The preacher should be fully confident to preach any passage of the Bible, knowing that God's Word is used by God's Spirit to shape God's people into God's image.

But there's another sense in which some texts are illegitimate for preaching. "By 'text' we signify a meaningful portion of any given book understood as part of that book and its overall message," Graeme Goldsworthy says. "Simply isolating a few words or a sentence from its real and immediate context does not qualify."[3]

In short, a legitimate preaching text is a complete unit of thought. Sidney Greidanus concurs with Goldsworthy, writing, "Whether short or long, a preaching-text ought to be a literary unit."[4]

In order to determine the boundaries of a literary unit, it's helpful to know the text's genre. If the genre is law, a literary unit could be as small as a single sentence, though context will often show that multiple laws have been grouped together. For example, you could legitimately cover all the Ten Commandments in one sermon, or spend an entire sermon focusing on one of the ten.

If the genre is narrative, the story forms a literary unit. If you were to break up a lengthy story into multiple sermons, you would still need to preach each sermon in light of the whole story in order to guard against misinterpretation (e.g., the Samson narrative in Judges 13–16).

If the genre is poetry, then the stanza is the smallest literary unit. Rarely, though, does a stanza stand in isolation from its surroundings. For instance, you could preach Jonah 2:9 alone, which ends with the famous declaration that "salvation belongs to the LORD." But it would probably be better to preach the entire poetic section (2:1–10). If you survey the text carefully, paying attention to genre, you'll have little trouble determining appropriate boundaries for the preaching text.

But literary boundaries aren't the only important factor in selecting a text. Believe it or not, the calendar is important, too! It's beneficial to select your text sooner rather than later. Some preachers wait to select their preaching text until the weekend, praying for the Spirit to lead them to the right message. Certainly, the Holy Spirit is gracious to help us prepare a "Saturday Night Special" when that's all the time we have to work with, but this approach isn't recommended. After all, the Spirit who helps the anxious preacher on Saturday night is the same Spirit who can help the preacher earlier in the week, or even several weeks or months in advance.

I know a pastor who not only plans his preaching calendar months in advance of the sermon, but who manuscripts his sermon two weeks before preaching it. Is this pastor a mere mortal? He's more like the Northern Hairy-Nosed Wombat—a rare species, indeed!

Whether we lack the time, the self-discipline, or even the capacity, most of us won't be ready to preach a brand-new sermon two weeks ahead of schedule. That's okay. But with just a little effort, most us will find that we can at least select our texts several weeks in advance. This allows both the preacher and the congregation to meditate on the passage days or even weeks ahead of the Sunday gathering. Make the calendar your friend.

My practice over the years has been to alternate preaching between the Old and New Testaments, making sure to cover the different sections and genres of Scripture. I preach expositional sermons from both a big picture "satellite view" and a more detailed "street view." After twenty years of preaching and teaching at the church I serve as Senior Pastor, this approach has enabled me to preach series of varying lengths through twenty-five books of the Old Testament.[5]

*Exegete the Preaching Text
in Its Old Testament Context*

Once you've selected a legitimate preaching text, the task of exegesis begins. The goal of exegesis is to discern the author's intended meaning as revealed in the text itself. The functional question we must answer is this: "What is the main point of the passage in its Old Testament context?" Any interpretation will fail if the preacher cannot discern what God is emphasizing in the text.

Step One: Text

*What is the main point of the passage
in its Old Testament context?*

To be clear, the meaning of a text isn't found in the author's mind apart from the text, or in the reader's mind according to what one desires the text to say. Meaning is found in what can be perceived in the text itself. God has revealed in written form what He intends to communicate. His words are intelligible and purposeful, making exegesis possible. With a little study, we can understand the point of what God has revealed. What a gift we have in the Bible!

What follows is a five-point sketch of the exegetical process.

1. Read thoroughly. Discerning the point of a text begins with reading the text carefully, then re-reading it, then re-re-reading it, then re-re-re- . . . you get the idea. I heard about one pastor who reads his preaching text fifty times before working on his sermon. Another Hairy-Nosed Wombat! Whether or not you read the text fifty times or half-a-dozen, there really is no substitute for immersing yourself in your text. Thorough reading is the foundational step in exegesis.

2. Observe details. While immersing yourself in the text, you'll begin to make numerous observations. From a wide-angle perspective, the main emphasis of the preaching passage will begin to emerge. Then, as you slowly zoom in, the details of the passage will refine your understanding of the main point. In narratives, for example, it's vital to notice details such as structural cues, conflict and resolution, and emphasis in dialogue. In law codes, you'll want to observe the grammar of each sentence, how each sentence relates to the sentences around it, the repetition of words, and any thematic arrangement. In poetry, be sure to take note of the parallelism in each stanza, and how the stanzas combine to emphasize a point. Also pay attention to the plethora of word pictures; they pervade Hebrew poetry and are brilliant devices for conveying meaning. If you let them, the biblical writers will turn your ears into eyes so that you can see their message. Regardless of genre, observe the details.

3. Understand context. You'll want to sharpen your focus on the main point by relating the text to its broader context within the book, to the covenant it reflects, and to its place within the history of the Old Testament. Take Ruth, for example. What's the significance of Ruth's nationality in the larger story of the Old Testament? How did Boaz know what procedure to follow in order to marry her? What's noteworthy about the book opening with the phrase "in the days when the judges ruled" and closing with the word "David"? Answering these broader contextual questions leads the interpreter to ponder the story of Ruth in light of the Law, of Israel's need for a godly king, and of the inclusion of the nations in the promises of God. It turns out that the book of Ruth isn't a dating manual for singles; rather, it's a significant movement in the history of redemption. The meaning of the text becomes richer when understood in its Old Testament context.

4. Use helps. Study resources are helpful tools for the exegetical process. Word study resources and dictionaries of historical and cultural backgrounds can be valuable in the early stages. However, I agree with the counsel of many who recommend using interpretive commentaries later in the process rather than earlier. You'll build greater confidence in interpretation when you've arrived at the main point of the text through your own study, only to discover that the commentaries refine your conclusion without fundamentally altering it.

5. Pray consistently. I've saved prayer for last not as an afterthought but as an exclamation point. When should the preacher pray for help in understanding God's Word? He should pray at the start of the exegetical process as he selects a text and begins reading it. He should pray as he makes observations about the text. He should pray as he seeks to understand the text in context. He should pray as he consults study resources. He should pray until he feels confident that he has identified the intended emphasis of the text. In summary, the preacher should pray throughout the exegetical process.

Imagine you've just read a complex novel, like Dostoevsky's *The Brothers Karamazov*. If you had the choice of participating in a discussion group or interacting with Dostoevsky himself, which would you choose? Which conversation would yield more insight into the meaning of the characters and their actions? While the group discussion might be enjoyable and even illuminating, it wouldn't compare to the author explaining his meaning.

Through prayer, we converse with the author of Scripture. God inspired His Word through the Spirit, and through the Spirit God illuminates our minds to understand that Word. "Open my eyes," the Psalmist prayed, "that I may behold wondrous things out of your law" (Ps. 119:18). The preacher should pray this way.

READY TO PREACH A SYNAGOGUE SERMON

So, select a legitimate text and exegete it in its Old Testament context. That's step one. Now, let's imagine that you've performed this step well. Good job!

But I've got some sobering news: you aren't yet ready to prepare your sermon. Your hermeneutical task isn't finished, unless of course you're a Jewish preacher preparing to preach in the synagogue. Another interpretive step must be taken if you are to be a Christian preacher.

Sadly, many preachers and teachers move directly from Old Testament exegesis to contemporary application. In doing so, they bypass the critical step of understanding the text's fulfillment in Christ. Don't make that mistake! Everything about the Old Testament flows to and through Jesus. You must be able to answer how He bears upon the main point of your text.

Until you can answer that question, you aren't ready to preach Christ—which leads us to the subject of the next chapter.

4

Fulfillment in Christ

Y ou probably remember the game Twister. Twister's board was a large vinyl mat with four rows of colored dots—red, yellow, blue, and green. The spinner determined the color on which the players had to place one of their hands or feet, with no one putting their hand or foot on the same dot. After just a few spins, the players became hilariously contorted while reaching over, under, and around each other, trying not to fall and be eliminated.

In moving from the TEXT to CHRIST, must the preacher play an interpretive game of Twister? Many preachers have certainly done so. Bryan Chapell provides a couple of amusing examples:

> Such interpreters may tell us things like the wood of Noah's ark symbolizes the wood of the cross. Or they may stretch a bit further and suggest that the wood of the ark was made of "gopher" wood, and that is supposed to remind us of the resurrection—since gophers live in the ground and Jesus came up out of the ground.[1]

Here's some good news: we don't need to be so imaginative in preaching Jesus. We don't have to contort the text to make a connection to Christ. We can put away the game of Old Testament Twister.

STEP TWO: CHRIST

The path between the text and Christ is not found in a Twister hermeneutic. Our goal instead is to understand how the text is fulfilled in Jesus.

Imagine you're preparing to preach about the fall of Adam in Genesis 3. Your sermon might analyze the anatomy of temptation and offer encouragement about how to succeed where Adam and Eve failed. That's not bad. But will you offer such encouragement in light of Christ? If so, how? What does Jesus have to do with the temptation of Adam and Eve? How does His life, death, and resurrection *fulfill* this story?

TEXT	CHRIST	US
Exegesis	Fulfillment	
Main Point	Gospel	
Jewish Sermon	Christological Sermon	

Or maybe you're preaching on the Ten Commandments, and your text for Sunday is the fourth commandment: "Remember the Sabbath day, to keep it holy" (Ex. 20:8–11). Do you preach this command as binding on the church today? You'll likely make some modifications—such as applying the command to Sunday instead of Saturday, or reassuring the church that enjoying certain forms of entertainment on Sunday is okay. But on what authority will you change *any* aspect of this command? Furthermore, what does the Sabbath have to do with Jesus? In what way does He *fulfill* it? We must grapple with these questions if we want to preach the Sabbath command as Christian pastors rather than old covenant rabbis or contemporary life coaches.

Or consider the famous prophetic promise of Jeremiah: "For I know the plans I have for you, declares the LORD, plans for welfare and not for evil, to give you a future and a hope" (29:11). Does this promise to the Jewish people in exile apply to everyone today? Only to Christians? Only to American Christians? Truly, truly, I say unto you, there are more bad ways of handling this verse than there are hairs on a cat! Before we apply this promise indiscriminately, even to the church, we must first understand how it relates to Jesus. How is this promise *fulfilled* in Christ?

> **Step Two: CHRIST**
>
> *How is the main point of the passage fulfilled in Christ?*

In Step One, we asked, "What is the main point of the passage in its Old Testament context?" In Step Two, our functional question builds on the first: "How is the main point of the passage fulfilled in Christ?" Until the preacher can answer the fulfillment question, he isn't ready to preach. In fact, until the preacher can answer the fulfillment question, he ought not preach. He doesn't yet understand his text. Besides, if we aren't going to preach Christ and what it means to live in Him, then why exactly are we preaching?

Thankfully, answering the fulfillment question isn't as hard as one might suspect because every answer falls in one or more of six categories: (1) prophetic promise, (2) ethical instruction, (3) fallen humanity, (4) typological revelation, (5) narrative progression, or (6) theological theme. My aim in this chapter is to explain each of these categories.

READING OVER JESUS' SHOULDER

To help you determine the category of your text—and, therefore, the most natural path for you to follow on the way to Christ—it might be helpful to imagine reading your text over Jesus' shoulder. How would He have understood its fulfillment?

I wish to draw your attention to an obvious but overlooked fact that can spark your imagination and improve your interpretive ability. It may even enliven your sense of wonder in Jesus as a person. Here it is: Jesus read the Old Testament. He heard the Scriptures taught every Sabbath. He stood over the wooden desk at the synagogue and read them for Himself. He meditated on them, memorized them, and made them central to His life and teaching.

And here's what makes this obvious but overlooked fact both relevant and remarkable: Jesus read the Old Testament *to see Himself*! He read it knowing how He would fulfill every bit of it. You and I apply a flawed hermeneutic when we seek to move directly from the Old Testament to our own lives, as if the Old Testament is not only for us but about us. But Jesus can apply our faulty hermeneutic accurately. The Old Testament is about *Him*, so He interpreted it rightly when He saw Himself in it.

This remarkable fact has led me closer to Jesus as I read the Old Testament. I'm indebted to Christopher Wright for helping me observe the obvious, and whose own feelings of awe I have come to share:

> In reading the Hebrew Scriptures I am handling something that gives me a closer common link with Jesus than any archaeological artifact could do. For these are the words *he* read. These were the stories he knew. These were the songs he sang. These were the depths of wisdom and revelation and prophecy that shaped his whole view of "life, the universe and everything." This is where he found his insights into the mind of his Father God. Above all, this is where he found the shape of his own identity and the goal of his own mission. In short, the deeper you go into understanding the Old Testament, the closer you come to the heart of Jesus.[2]

Fellow pastors and teachers, I hope the thought of Jesus reading the Old Testament will bring you closer to His heart. Before the Old Testament was yours to apply, it was Jesus' to fulfill. So read it with Him, over His shoulder. Learn to read it *about Him* the way He would have read it *about Himself*. Instead of asking only, "How do I read this text?" ask yourself also, "How would Jesus have read this text?"

For those of you who are nervous about the language of reading over Jesus' shoulder, let me assure you that I'm being metaphorical, not mystical. I'm simply saying that reading toward fulfillment in Christ was how Jesus Himself read the text. He had a way of understanding His own life in every passage He pondered, and so we must try to interpret the text how He would have. The following six categories will help us do that.

PROPHETIC PROMISE:

The Identity of Jesus in Promises and Prophecies

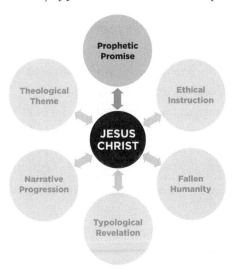

The category of Prophetic Promise is the easiest and least controversial way of seeing Christ in the Old Testament. Numerous Old

Testament texts contain divine promises of a coming Savior. We tend to think these messianic promises are found primarily in the Prophets, and many of them are. However, redemptive promises are also scattered throughout the Law and the Writings.

For example, consider these prophetic promises, all of which are fulfilled in Christ:

From the Law:
- The offspring of woman, who will bruise the serpent's head (Gen. 3:15; cf. Gal. 4:4).
- The offspring of Abraham, in whom God will establish an eternal covenant (Gen. 17:7; cf. Gal. 3:16).
- A star coming out of Jacob (Num. 24:17; cf. Matt. 2:2).
- A prophet like Moses, raised up from among Israel (Deut. 18:15; cf. Acts 3:22–26).

From the Prophets:
- The offspring of David, who will rule as King forever (2 Sam. 7:12–13; cf. Matt. 1:1).
- The Suffering Servant, dying as a substitute for sinners (Isa. 52:13–53:12; cf. Acts 8:32–35).
- The initiator of a new covenant (Jer. 31:31–34; cf. Luke 22:20).
- A ruler, born in Bethlehem (Micah 5:2; cf. Matt. 2:6).

From the Writings:
- One whose flesh and soul will never die (Ps. 16:8–11; cf. Acts 2:24–32).
- The Lord and eternal priest (Ps. 110; cf. Acts 2:34–36; Heb. 7:15–25).
- One like a son of man, coming on the clouds (Dan. 7:13–14; cf. Matt. 24:30).
- An eternally loved Son of God (1 Chron. 17:13; cf. Heb. 1:5).

These promises and dozens more like them are inherently forward-looking. They raise the interpreter's eyes to a future horizon. The future horizon may begin in the Old Testament itself, where the prophetic promise is shown to have partial fulfillment. For example, we see partial fulfillment of Psalm 2's "my Son" prophecy in the kings of Judah. We shouldn't neglect to understand prophetic promises like this within their Old Testament context, as we learned in Step One. But, like scaling a peak only to discover a larger mountain in the distance, we must eventually see how every prophetic promise moves forward through redemptive history to its complete fulfillment in the person and work of Jesus Christ. So, in Psalm 2, we understand Jesus to be the Son whom God installs as King on Zion.

Many prophetic promises are cited in the New Testament. These references are like candy for the preacher. What could inspire more confidence in Old Testament interpretation than the New Testament showing how a text is fulfilled in Christ? But even in the absence of a New Testament quotation or allusion, we can still perceive a clear connection to Jesus. For example, the interpreter is right to see the experience of Christ's suffering on the cross described throughout Psalm 22, even though the New Testament doesn't allude to every verse from the psalm. We also know that Jesus is the ultimate referent in Isaiah's servant prophecies. Once we understand Jesus as the Servant in Isaiah 52–53, we're inclined to trace the other servant prophecies to Him as well.

Jesus interpreted the Bible this way. Can you imagine what it must have been like for Jesus to read and hear the prophetic promises, understanding that they were speaking of Him? I know a woman who discovered her elderly mother's old journal tucked away in some long-forgotten things. She described the surreal experience of reading her mother's own words, written decades before, about raising her little girl—*about raising her*. What she read in the journal influenced how she began to look at herself, despite all the years that had passed.

How much more influential would the words of God about His

Son have been for Jesus! Certainly Jesus the boy, and Jesus the young man, and Jesus the adult would have been profoundly shaped by the prophetic promises in the Scriptures. His self-identity would have been clearly shown in understanding Himself to be the offspring of woman, of Abraham, and of David; of being the promised King who would one day rule the nations; of being the Priest who would atone for sin once for all through the sacrifice of His own body; of being the beloved Son of God.

How was it that Jesus' confidence in His identity and mission was so clear? At least part of the explanation is that His Father had shaped His identity through scriptural words of prophetic promise.

Does your preaching text include a prophetic promise? Then preach Christ as its fulfillment.

ETHICAL INSTRUCTION:
The Lifestyle of Jesus in Law and Wisdom

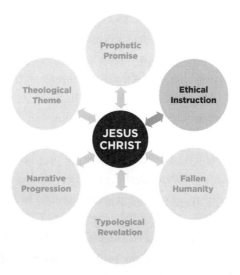

Ethical instruction is another straightforward way of understanding how a text is fulfilled in Jesus. In fact, this path between the text and Jesus is so plain that you may have missed it—just like I did. Let me explain.

Ethical instructions are all over the Old Testament. But we find them most prominently in the law code and in wisdom literature (e.g., Exodus, Leviticus, Numbers, Deuteronomy, Psalms, Proverbs, Ecclesiastes). Why here? Because God is teaching His people how to live. He's giving them commands and precepts and guidance that He intends for them to follow.

What do these ethical instructions have to do with Jesus? The answer is simple: Jesus fulfilled them! All those laws? Jesus kept them— Jesus is *the* lawkeeper (Matt. 5:17). All of God's instruction in wisdom? Jesus embodied it perfectly—Jesus is *the* wise man (1 Cor. 1:30). Every bit of ethical instruction in the Old Testament has been fulfilled in Jesus.

What an exciting realization! When you read God's ethical instructions to His people, you're learning about Jesus. You're learning how His mind and heart were formed. You're learning what information He used to calculate His decisions. You're learning how He understood sin and righteousness. You're learning the background to everything He taught. Ethical instructions show us the shape of Jesus' life.

So be sure to read these ethical instructions over Jesus' shoulder. Consider, for example, the command, "You shall not commit adultery" (Deut. 5:18). Jesus read and understood this command as ethical instruction that applied to Him, one that must be fulfilled as part of His obedience to His Father. It shaped Him as a faithful man. It influenced how He would teach, which is apparent in His emphasis on sexual purity in the Sermon on the Mount (Matt. 5:27–30). Ultimately, Jesus' keeping of the seventh commandment contributed to His righteous life, which He would sacrifice on the cross for sexually corrupt people.

Or consider these wisdom sayings from Proverbs: "Answer not a fool according to his folly, lest you be like him yourself. Answer a fool according to his folly, lest he be wise in his own eyes" (Prov. 26:4–5).

Jesus read these instructions and took them to heart. He pondered how to interact carefully with foolish people, challenging them with the truth without descending to their level. Many well-intentioned Christians struggle to apply this wisdom, making compromises in their words or actions while trying to reach their lost friends with the gospel. Yet here's another point at which to admire Jesus: He never compromised Himself or the truth in His interactions with unbelievers. We can admire His wise interaction with all sorts of unbelievers, from curious rulers to immoral women to recalcitrant crowds (John 3–5). Jesus fulfilled all wisdom by living out the wisdom of God.

These two examples—sexual purity and conversational wisdom—raise a question about the relative usefulness of ethical instruction in preaching Christ from the Old Testament. Though every law and every wisdom saying was fulfilled in Jesus, they won't all be equally useful in the sermon. For example, Jesus never plowed a field with an ox and donkey together, nor did He wear clothing blended with wool and linen (Deut. 22:10–11). His obedience to these laws provides us with clarifying facts about our Lord. It's encouraging to remember that Jesus fulfilled these laws in letter and in spirit as a necessary part of His righteousness. However, it's difficult to imagine a sermon in which these particular instructions become the main point of the message.

On the other hand, when Jesus' obedience to ethical instruction is observable, and when you can discern that emphasizing it clarifies how we ought to live today as Christians, then this path of fulfillment offers an appropriate and edifying way to preach Christ.

More must be said about applying Old Testament ethics to our own lives. Piles of books have been written on the subject. I will save that discussion for Step Three, in which we move from fulfillment in Christ to how we live in union with Him. For now, though, don't be myopic like I was—don't miss the astonishingly plain connection between ethical instruction and the person of Christ.

Most people have heard of Arthur Conan Doyle's renowned detective, Sherlock Holmes. Less familiar is the literary character upon which Sherlock was based, C. Auguste Dupin. Dupin was created by Edgar Allen Poe, who wrote three short stories featuring this Sherlockian prototype. In one of the stories, "The Purloined Letter," Dupin recovers a stolen letter hidden in a thief's hotel suite. Dupin's recovery astonished the police, who had meticulously searched for the letter. They had gone so far as to look between every page of every book, to take a microscope to all the furniture and every floorboard, and to probe the chair cushions with fine long needles. Every square inch of the thief's rooms had been scrutinized by the police.

So how had the stolen letter eluded them? *Because it was out in the open the entire time.* Knowing the police's methods, the thief had placed the valuable letter in an open stack of mail, thus hiding it in plain sight. But, knowing the mind of the thief, Dupin easily recovered it.

I feel a bit like the police in Poe's story. For years I missed the obvious connection between ethical instruction and Christ, even though it was hiding in plain sight. I failed to consider how Jesus had fulfilled Scripture's ethical instructions in His own life and teaching. Now I try to be more like Dupin, seeing the path of fulfillment that's right there in the open. As you do the same, your own worship of Jesus will be enriched and your hearers will be edified.

Does your preaching text contain ethical instruction? If so, it's teaching you about Jesus. Jesus followed those instructions perfectly and interpreted them fully. So don't bypass Him on your way to personal application. Don't miss the opportunity to hold up the life and teaching of Jesus for everyone to admire.

FALLEN HUMANITY:
The Burden of Jesus in Sin and Suffering

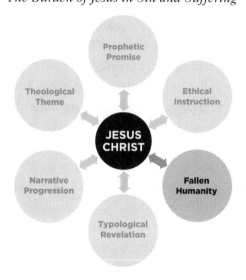

I've lived in Tennessee most of my life, and I'll never forget a certain TV commercial that aired when I was a child. I don't know if commercials have names, but I've always referred to this one as "Tennessee Trash." The commercial featured a scruffy man in a dirty white tank top, driving a beat-up convertible. As he drove, the man tossed garbage out of his car and onto the road. Aluminum cans, glass bottles, paper scraps—you name it. They flew from his car like fireballs exploding out of a Roman candle. At one point, the man stopped to kick a filthy rolled-up mattress out of the front seat! All the while, a twangy song played in the background: "Lawd, there ain't no lower class than Tennessee trash."

The commercial ended with the car fading out of sight, litter covering every bit of the highway. Then, these final words appeared on the screen: "We have met the enemy, and he is us!"

"Tennessee Trash" was part of a statewide anti-littering initiative. It's also an apt metaphor for fallen humanity. We all drive down the highway of life, littering our relationships and our world with disobedience to God. The garbage within is tossed out all around us. We are a wreck, and we are wreckers.

Virtually every page of Scripture testifies to this fallen condition. Consider the sin and suffering just in the opening chapters of the Bible. In the so-called universal history of the world prior to the call of Abram (Gen. 1–11), we see Adam the law-breaker, Cain the brother-killer, the sons of God as lust-indulgers, Noah the wine-abuser, Ham the father-mocker, and the whole earth as Babel-builders. And that's just the beginning of the Bible!

After the call of Abram, things don't improve. From Genesis 12 onward, we see jealousy, deceit, incest, grumbling, sickness, disease, barrenness, drought, famine, prostitution, adultery, homosexuality, and all manner of covenant unfaithfulness. There's blood from Abel to Zechariah (Luke 11:51)—and a host of litter in between. "Tennessee Trash" got it right: we have met the enemy, and he is us.

Thankfully, each instance of fallen humanity provides fertile ground for preaching Christ. When the focus of the text is sin and suffering—whether seen in acts of faithlessness or disobedience or broken relationships or disaster or exile or death—the path to Christ is wide and clear. "Here's another example of why we need a Savior!" the preacher can exclaim. "Here's why God sent His Son into the world!"

Fallen humanity shows us our need for Jesus. "The saying is trustworthy and deserving of full acceptance, that Christ Jesus came into the world to save sinners" (1 Tim. 1:15). Jesus fulfills the grim realities of the fall by becoming a curse for us (Gal. 3:13). In His crucifixion and resurrection, He atones for sin and triumphs over evil. The cross and the empty tomb signal the coming destruction of the world, the flesh, and the devil. What a joy for the preacher to proclaim that, in Christ, the horrible effects of the fall are being rolled back, and all things are being made new (2 Cor. 5:17; Eph. 2:1–10; Col. 2:13–15). What a joy to preach of the coming day when loud voices in heaven will announce,

"The kingdom of the world has become the kingdom of our Lord and of his Christ, and he shall reign forever and ever" (Rev. 11:15).

Bryan Chapell's well-known emphasis on the Fallen Condition Focus fits within this category of fulfillment. In his outstanding book *Christ-Centered Preaching*, Chapell argues that all of Scripture exhibits the fallen condition of humanity. Every bit of the Bible instructs our deficient thinking, corrects our errant behavior, and trains us for righteousness through faith in Jesus Christ (2 Tim. 3:15–17). In other words, every passage reveals not only our need for salvation, but how God's grace in Christ actually meets that need. Chapell's pudding story memorably makes the point:

> When I was a child, my mother spent an afternoon making a special chocolate pudding for our family of eight. When she brought the fabulous dessert to the dinner table, however, the impact was marred by the deep imprint of a child's finger in the middle of the bowl. Someone had sneaked an early taste. My mother asked, "Who?" No one fessed up, but that did not stop my mother's investigation. She simply began matching the index finger of the six children to the hole in the top of the pudding until she found the digit that fit (it wasn't mine). The impression not only revealed the pudding's incompleteness but also identified the one who would fill the hole. God's imprinting of our incompleteness on a passage of Scripture does not merely demonstrate an aspect of our fallenness; it also reveals the nature and character of the One who can make us whole.[3]

Our lives and all of God's good creation have been marred by the deep imprint of sin. And yet, God's redeeming grace has come to us in the person and work of Christ—and it fills the hole. Christ is the solution to fallen humanity.

Jesus undoubtedly felt the burden of human need as He read His Old Testament. He knew what He had come into the world to accomplish (Matt. 16:21; Heb. 10:5–6). The cross would have loomed ever larger in His mind as He considered the biblical accounts of sin and suffering. With every story of faithlessness and disobedience, with every instance of suffering due to the curse, with every law broken and every proverb shunned, the burden of Jesus' bloody mission became palpable. He was a dead man walking, facing a death sentence for sins not His own. Jesus' reading of Scripture prepared Him for this. His mission to die as an atoning sacrifice was deepened by the Bible. The same passages that impress us with our need for a Savior impressed Jesus with His burden to save.

So, when the main point of your preaching text is focused on fallen humanity, you have a clear path to Jesus. Sin and suffering show our need for Christ's redeeming death and life-giving resurrection. Wherever there's sin and suffering, there's need for the work of Christ. As the song so beautifully says, "He comes to make His blessings flow far as the curse is found." Where the curse is, there Christ shall be.

Whether you're preaching the fall of Adam, Korah's rebellion, Israel's defeat at Ai, the death of Uzzah, Job's suffering, or even a series through Proverbs, you will find it easy to move from those texts to our own sinfulness to the comfort of the gospel. Jesus is the Savior who died and rose again to deal with our pervasive problem of sin and suffering.

TYPOLOGICAL REVELATION:
The Shadow of Jesus in Pictures and Patterns

Of all the ways Jesus fulfills the Old Testament, typology raises the most questions. And if typology isn't employed well, it raises the most eyebrows, too! Typology is hotly debated, all the way down to the word itself.

Have you seen those road construction signs that have a flashing orange light on top? Imagine one of those signs right here. We should proceed carefully, but we must proceed.

Regarding typology, every preacher should wrestle with three key questions:

- What is a type?
- What are some examples of types in the Bible?
- Is it okay to see a type when there is no cross-reference to identify it?

What is a type? Let's begin with a definition—or two or three definitions! First, and most basically, a type is simply a pattern. A type is theology in picture form. As David Murray puts it, "It's a kind of visual theology. God pictured the truth to preach the truth."[4]

A bit more expansively, a type is a *shadow* whose greater reality is the *substance* (Col. 2:16–17). The shadow could be a person, an event, or an institution in the Old Testament that God designed to prefigure something greater than itself. In reference to preaching Jesus, we're talking about a shadow whose substance is Christ.

Third, and most precisely, a type is "a real person, place, object, or event that God ordained to act as a predictive pattern or resemblance of Jesus' person and work." Again, Murray supplies a helpful definition, unpacking it as follows:

- *A type is a real person, place, object, or event:* it is true, real, and factual—not a made-up allegory.
- *That God ordained:* it resembled Jesus' person and work not by mere coincidence but by divine plan.
- *To act as a predictive pattern or resemblance:* the same truth is found in the Old Testament picture and the New Testament fulfillment.
- *Of Jesus' person and work:* the truth in the picture is enlarged, heightened, and clarified in the fulfillment.[5]

If you understand these three definitions, congratulations! You have a rudimentary but solid grasp of biblical typology. Of course, we'll be accused of oversimplifying if we stop here. So let's keep going. Let's bring visual theology into sharper focus by looking at some biblical examples.

What are some examples of types in the Bible? One of the first and most fundamental types in Scripture is none other than the first man, Adam:

Yet death reigned from Adam to Moses, even over those whose sinning was not like the transgression of Adam, who was a type of the one who was to come. . . . For if, because of one man's trespass, death reigned through that one man, much more will those who receive the abundance of grace and the free gift of righteousness reign in life through the one man Jesus Christ.

Therefore, as one trespass led to condemnation for all men, so one act of righteousness leads to justification and life for all men. For as by the one man's disobedience the many were made sinners, so by the one man's obedience the many will be made righteous. (Rom. 5:14, 17–19)

Using our definitions above, notice that Adam is a real person, whom God ordained to function as a "type of the one who was to come." In other words, Adam was a predictive pattern for Christ. Both men stand at the head of a stream of humanity—Adam for all who are condemned and dying, and Jesus for all who are justified and living. In the contrast between the two men, we notice a perfecting of the type. Adam trespassed, but Jesus acted righteously. Adam disobeyed and made many to be sinners, but Jesus obeyed and made many to be righteous. Such a movement from the imperfect to the perfect is common in typology. The shadow gives way to the substance!

Special days provide another example of types. As the apostle Paul teaches,

Therefore let no one pass judgment on you in questions of food and drink, or with regard to a festival or a new moon or a Sabbath. These are a shadow of the things to come, but the substance belongs to Christ. (Col. 2:16–17)

Note here that the apostle Paul provides us with the language of "shadow" and "substance." Paul points out, among other things, that the special days of the old covenant were shadows of Christ. In other words, God designed them to be suggestive shapes of a future reality, and Christ fulfills them by being in Himself the substance of all that they signified.

The temple and its sacrificial system are further examples of well-known types. Consider these words of Jesus and the writer of Hebrews:

Jesus answered them, "Destroy this temple, and in three days I will raise it up." The Jews then said, "It has taken forty-six years to build this temple, and will you raise it up in three days?" But he was speaking about the temple of his body. (John 2:19–21)

For since the law has but a shadow of the good things to come instead of the true form of these realities, it can never, by the same sacrifices that are continually offered every year, make perfect those who draw near. . . . For by a single offering [Christ] has perfected for all time those who are being sanctified. (Heb. 10:1, 14)

When Jesus read about temple worship and sacrifices, He saw Himself. If we were reading over His shoulder, we might hear Him say, "Here I am, sketched out in institutional form. Here's what I've come to fulfill." In His own life, death, and resurrection, Jesus understood that He was the substance of all that these institutions depicted. He was the embodiment of God's presence, the one in whom we meet with the Father, the final and perfect sacrifice for sinners.

The New Testament gives us numerous other examples of types: Melchizedek (Heb. 7:2–3); Moses (Acts 3:22); David (Matt. 1:1); Solomon (Luke 11:31); Jonah (Matt. 12:40–41); Israel (Matt. 2:13–15); the priesthood (Heb. 10:1–7), and others. Typological revelation is good ground for preaching Christ.

Is it okay to see a type when there is no biblical cross-reference to help identify it? The crux of the controversy surrounding typology lies here. How you answer depends largely on what you believe about the nature of typology. On one hand, if you believe types are shadows of Christ that God intentionally built into redemptive history (as defined above), you will be less inclined to see a type without some sort of biblical warrant. Scripture must interpret Scripture. Otherwise, how do you *know* that God intended this person, event, or institution to be a type?

On the other hand, if you believe types are less a part of the prophetic fabric of Scripture and more like gospel symbols that Jesus and the apostles overlaid on the Old Testament, you'll be more inclined to see a type without a cross-reference to validate it. Typology, according to this perspective, isn't so much about divine design as it is interpretive imagination.

There is more interpretive freedom with the latter approach, to be sure. There is also more interpretive danger. Many preachers have abused typology. You've probably heard *bad* typology before, like,

- "Nehemiah is rebuilding the city gates. One of those gates is called the Sheep Gate, which makes me think of shepherds, which reminds me of the good shepherd, which leads us to Jesus. The sheep gate is a type of Christ!"
- Or, "King Ahasuerus extended his golden scepter to Esther so that she could approach him. God must extend grace to us so that we can approach Him. Ahasuerus' golden scepter is a type of Christ!"
- Or (my personal favorite), "Balaam's donkey rebuked Balaam as a false teacher. Jesus rebuked false teachers. Balaam's donkey is a type of Christ!"

Penalty flags should be thrown for such typological shenanigans. Discerning a genuine type isn't an exercise in free association! But the million-dollar question is, "How do we *know* the sheep gate or the king's scepter or the prophet's donkey isn't a type of Christ?" Why shouldn't we consider examples like these to be legitimate? If typology is about using your imagination to turn Old Testament details into symbols of the gospel, then there really is no basis for ruling an interpretation out of bounds.

But typology isn't about interpretive imagination. The way we know that some passages are typological and others aren't—the only way we can know—is through biblical warrant. Scripture that must show us the shadows. And Scripture does! How? Through a strata of typological correspondence.

Like various layers of rock, Scripture has a strata of cross-references that enable the preacher to discern the presence of typology in the preaching passage.[6] **Explicit references** form the bedrock stratum. When a cross-reference explicitly identifies an element of the preaching text as a type, you can be confident in your typological interpretation. Additionally, once the typology of a person, event, or institution has been explicitly established, you are justified in exploring the range of typological connections between that type and Christ, even when the preaching passage itself has no cross-reference.

Consider David, for instance. Scripture teaches us that David is a type of Christ, so we are right to discern shadows of Christ in the life of David, despite not having a cross-reference for every specific connection. Many have detected a foreshadowing of Jesus in David's slaying of Goliath; or in David graciously giving Mephibosheth a seat at the king's table; or in many of David's psalms functioning as a prophetic picture of Christ. Cross-references aren't needed for each of these connections, because Scripture has already established David as a type. The connections fall within the extended range of David's typological significance.

By contrast, whereas the Bible explicitly establishes David as a type of Christ, it doesn't say the same of Saul or Jonathan or Absalom. The preacher, therefore, should rightfully be wary of seeing in them a type of Christ. Important biblical characters and incidents may in fact resemble Jesus on occasion, but absent an explicit reference establishing their typological significance, one cannot be absolutely certain.

A secondary stratum of cross-references is **probable allusions.** Whereas explicit references are unmistakable, probable allusions are slightly less so. Yet Jesus and the apostles seem frequently to allude to Old Testament passages, often in a typological way. In John 3:16, for example, God's "only Son" likely alludes to Isaac in Genesis 22. John sees the almost-sacrificed Isaac as a type that is fulfilled in Christ, who as God's only Son would not be spared from death. Samuel also seems to function as a type of Christ, as indicated by the connection Luke makes between the two growing boys (Luke 2:52; 1 Sam. 2:26). Interestingly, Luke also seems to view Elijah as a type of Christ. In Luke 4–9, various aspects of the prophet's ministry echo within Jesus' own ministry—from their each being dispatched to a Gentile widow, to the raising of a widow's son from the dead, to allusions of fire being called down from heaven, to both of them being "taken up" to heaven.

This is just a sampling of numerous probable typological allusions between the New Testament and the Old. What a call for us to know our Bibles well, so that we don't miss them! The certainty with which we preach a type based on an allusion may be slightly less than when our text is linked to an explicit reference. But if the allusion is likely, we can preach Christ in faith.

The shallowest stratum of cross-references is **subtle connections.** Subtle typological connections aren't explicit, nor are they allusions. Yet their thematic or covenantal significance as a pattern for Christ is highlighted elsewhere in the Bible, outside the preaching text. Take Joseph, for example, who is given extensive focus in Genesis. To my knowledge, no explicit reference or probable allusion links Joseph to Jesus. Yet in his last sermon before being stoned, Stephen traces covenantal history through Joseph as a rejected figure through whom God brings redemption (Acts 7:9–16). The typological connection is subtle, yet it's there. Joseph's life seems intended by God to foreshadow the suffering and salvation of Jesus, as did the lives of Moses and the prophets after him (Acts 7:20–53). Scripture makes other subtle connections as well—connections that aren't mere coincidental resemblances to Jesus, read back into the text. The shadows really are present, divinely designed and validated by Scripture itself.

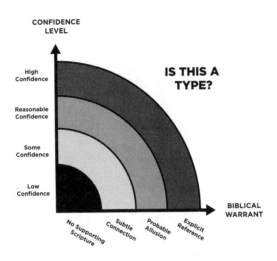

When Jesus read the Old Testament, He saw shadows of His own life, death, and resurrection; He saw the kingdom He came to establish. The Father had providentially arranged history to include these pictures and patterns, all of which would be fulfilled in His Son. Our own understanding of Jesus will be impoverished if we disregard this sharply debated but thoroughly biblical category of fulfillment. For the sake of preaching Christ, every preacher must seek to discern the presence of legitimate typology. We don't want to see shadows that aren't there, but we sure don't want to miss the ones that are. Being alert to explicit references, probable allusions, and subtle connections will help.

Is there a type of Christ in the text? Don't be afraid to preach Jesus as its fulfillment.

NARRATIVE PROGRESSION:
The Backstory of Jesus in Threat and Resolution

It's hard to talk about backstories without thinking of superheroes. Superhero origin movies have been wildly popular. Where did Batman come from? What was his family like? His upbringing? What was the defining moment, or moments, in his past that made him who he was? We pack out theaters to hear answers to these questions, rows and rows of amateur psychologists in reclining chairs, probing the depths of popcorn buckets and our favorite characters' formative histories.

But our fascination with backstory isn't limited to fictional superheroes. Often when we come across someone interesting, influential, or eccentric, we want to know more about them. We want to understand what shaped them into the people that they are.

Of course, Jesus has a backstory—and what a backstory it is! Announced by angels, born of a virgin, laid in a manger, visited by shepherds and wise men, hunted by a king, swept off to Egypt, raised in a small Galilean town. But there's more to Jesus' backstory than these

New Testament details. The New Testament itself, as a matter of fact, would have us go all the way back to Genesis (and beyond) to understand Jesus' backstory: "In the beginning was the Word, and the Word was with God, and the Word was God" (John 1:1).

As the eternal Son of God, Jesus' backstory stretches into eternity past and encompasses everything from the creation of the world to His birth in Bethlehem. In other words, the entire Old Testament is the backstory of Jesus.

In learning the backstory of Jesus, we must pay attention not merely to historical details but to the *storied* details of the Old Testament. Through narrative progression, we see how the redemptive story line of the Old Testament flows toward Christ. Jesus fulfills the big story of the Bible. He's the point of a story that starts in the garden of Genesis and ends in the Garden City of Revelation.

Much of the Law, all the Former Prophets, and a portion of the Writings—Genesis through Esther in our English Bibles—is made up of stories. These stories record God's revelation as it progresses through time, following the plotline laid out in the covenant promises and eventually climaxing in Christ.

Unfortunately, it's easy to take these stories and move straight to contemporary application without seeking to understand their place in the flow of redemptive history. This blunder is the cause of so much Christless, moralistic preaching, not to mention the prosperity gospel heresy. We must stop making this mistake. Old Testament stories tell the history of Jesus, and the preacher who cares about preaching Christ will make the connection between the two.

In order to do this, we should ask ourselves, "How is this story important in the flow of redemptive history? How does it help us make progress toward Jesus?"

Take, for example, the story of Jacob and Esau. Theirs isn't a story merely about sibling rivalry but about how the covenant promise to Abraham will be passed on. The promise will be carried out through the younger son rather than the older. And to ratchet up the conflict, the younger son isn't exactly a paragon of virtue. The story raises the question: "How is God going to fulfill His promise through a younger brother and conniving deceiver like Jacob?" That's the *real* tension of the story, and the resolution of that tension will either jettison the gospel or move us one step closer to it. The world won't have Jesus if God's promise fails in Jacob. And so we preach about the sibling rivalry, but our sermon's main point is *not* that brothers and sisters ought to get along. Instead, we highlight how the rivalry between Jacob and Esau threatened the very future of Christ, and how God graciously and faithfully resolved that threat. We preach the Old Testament story as the backstory to the big Story.

Fulfillment in Christ through narrative progression also applies to the Former Prophets. For example, consider the conquest of Canaan. These stories aren't morality tales about having courage like Joshua so that God will enlarge the borders in your life. No, the conquest is about how God faithfully keeps His promise to establish a people for Himself in the land (Josh. 21:45). The promise is at stake. If God doesn't establish His people as He said He would, then God would be a liar and the world wouldn't have Jesus. So, in your sermons through the book of Joshua, call people to courageous faith in God's promises, encouraging them through the conquest of Canaan that God has *always* been faithful to keep His promises. Preach these Old Testament stories as the backstory to the big Story.

The story of Esther is similar. Esther isn't a morality tale about how the world needs strong women. Esther is about how God providentially orchestrates events to protect His people and secure His promise of redemption. Wonderfully, women are often key instruments in God's redemptive work in the world. We can highlight this fact and encourage women (and men) to trust God as Esther did. But the bigger picture comes into focus through Haman's threat against the Jews. If God's people are annihilated, then God's promises will utterly fail. Jesus' family tree will be cut down, and the world won't have Jesus. Talk about a defining moment in Jesus' history! So preach this Old Testament story as the backstory to the big Story.

You get the idea. The stories of the Old Testament tell the backstory of Jesus. They show how God works out His promises of redemption. They often pose a threat to God's covenant promises, and then show us how God resolves that threat so that His promise moves on— *all the way to its fulfillment in Christ.*

Jesus would have read these stories as His own backstory. He would have felt the unique threat each posed to His incarnate existence, and He would have celebrated as each was resolved through the faithfulness of His Father. The Old Testament's narrative rhythm—threat and resolution, threat and resolution, threat and resolution—surely spurred Jesus on under the looming threat of His crucifixion. Which previous threat in redemptive history had His Father failed to resolve? None? Then God most certainly would secure His promise in its climactic moment by raising His Son from the dead.

Don't move from historical narrative to contemporary application without looking ahead to Jesus. Be sure to grasp how the little stories of the text form the backstory of Jesus, who is the big story of the entire Bible.

THEOLOGICAL THEME:

The Preview of Jesus in God's Acts and Attributes

Some Old Testament passages have as their main point a theological theme whose fulfillment is found in Christ. The theme could have to do with justice, wrath, judgment, mercy, forgiveness, love, or holiness, just to name a few. When the focus of the text is a theological theme, the preacher needs to consider how the theme relates to the person and work of Christ.

More specifically, you'll find that theological themes often have to do with an act or an attribute of God. When God acts in salvation history or the text highlights one of His attributes, you're right to make a connection between that act or attribute and Jesus Himself. Jesus is, after all, "the image of the invisible God" (Col. 1:15). And, as John tells us, "No one has ever seen God; the only God, who is at the Father's side, he has made him known" (John 1:18). Therefore, to observe the acts and attributes of God in the Old Testament is to see a preview of Jesus, because Jesus reveals God in the flesh. Jesus *is* God-in-the-flesh!

Let's dig deeper into this idea by considering three Old Testament passages. Consider, for example, the story of Naboth's vineyard. Naboth isn't the main point of the story but serves as a backdrop for the wickedness of Ahab and Jezebel (1 Kings 21:25). Ahab and Jezebel aren't the main point of the story either but are themselves the backdrop for a surprising action of God that happens in the very last verse of the narrative. Following Ahab's completely unexpected change of heart, the Lord says to Elijah, "Have you seen how Ahab has humbled himself before me? Because he has humbled himself before me, I will not bring the disaster in his days; but in his son's days I will bring the disaster upon his house" (21:29).

This surprise ending highlights the point of the narrative: the Lord shows mercy to those who repent in the face of judgment. The story is designed, with its surprise ending, to make this point—a crucial point for Ahab, for idolatrous Israel, and for us all. It's a clear example of a theological theme. And nowhere in all of redemptive history will this theological theme be played out as clearly as in the gospel of Jesus Christ. The narrative of Naboth's vineyard is a preview of God's disposition toward those who humble themselves before the Savior. Jesus would've understood this theological theme as being a reflection of what God was going to do for people, ultimately, through the cross. His sacrificial death would be the basis of God's mercy toward repentant sinners.

Or consider, as another example, the most famous of the psalms. The opening verses of Psalm 23 portray the Lord as a shepherd. In redemptive history, how will the Lord most clearly reveal Himself as a shepherd? The answer is obvious—in Christ Jesus, of course! It's no coincidence that Jesus would call Himself the "good shepherd [who] lays down his life for the sheep" (John 10:11), or that the New Testament writers would refer to Jesus as "the chief Shepherd" (1 Peter 5:4) and "the great shepherd of the sheep" (Heb. 13:20). We aren't making typological connections or preaching in terms of messianic prophecy when we point to Jesus through Psalm 23. Rather, we're seeing how a particular theological theme fully blooms in Christ. We understand that the Father of Jesus is a shepherd, and that Jesus is the embodiment of the shepherding love of God.

The story in which God establishes a covenant with Abraham provides yet another opportunity to preach Christ through theological theme. When the Lord promises offspring to Abraham, the text tells us that Abraham "believed the LORD, and [the LORD] counted it to him as righteousness" (Gen. 15:6). Certainly, God's promise of offspring finds its fulfillment in Christ by way of prophetic promise—our first category of fulfillment. Jesus Himself is the offspring of Abraham (Gal. 3:16).

But what about Abraham's response to God's promise? Does Abraham's faith point us to Jesus? How so? Abraham's response of faith leads us to Christ not by way of prophetic promise but through theological theme. Here we have the doctrine of justification by faith. Paul will refer to Genesis 15:6 twice, on both occasions locating justification in the person of Christ (Rom. 3–4; Gal. 3). Now that the promised offspring has arrived, the doctrine of justification has become more specific. Justification through faith in God and in His promise is now justification through faith in Christ, who is the fulfillment of the promise. Grasping this doctrinal development is crucial. If you call people to follow Abraham's example of faith yet fail to show how justification is found in Christ, you will not have pointed your hearers to saving righteousness. The theological theme of justification is fulfilled in Jesus.

When the main point of an Old Testament passage is a theological theme—such as mercy in the face of judgment, or the care of God as a shepherd, or the basis on which God justifies a person—ask yourself how that theme finds expression or fulfillment in Jesus. To perceive a saving act or attribute of God is to see a preview of God-in-the-flesh, Jesus Christ. In those cases, preach God, but don't stop there. Preach Christ.

5

Case Studies in Fulfillment

In the last chapter I outlined six categories for understanding how the Old Testament is fulfilled in Christ:

- Prophetic Promise
- Ethical Instruction
- Fallen Humanity
- Typological Revelation
- Narrative Progression
- Theological Theme

Following one or more of these paths from TEXT to CHRIST is Step Two in the interpretive process. If every pen stroke of the Old Testament finds its fulfillment in Christ, then we must labor to understand all of it in light of Him.

My wife once bought a nice pair of sunglasses with interchangeable lenses. One set of lenses was for low light, one for medium light, and another for bright light. Depending on the level of sunlight, she would pop in the appropriate lenses. When interpreting the Old Testament, think of these six paths to Christ as interchangeable lenses. Select which lens to use depending on the passage's main point.

What if more than one lens seems to fit the text? It's been my observation that Christ often fulfills the preaching text in multiple ways. For example, I mentioned Joseph in the previous chapter. Depending on the focus of your preaching passage, such as Joseph being despised and rejected by his brothers, you might follow Stephen's cue in Acts and preach Joseph as a type of Christ. On the other hand, considering how the Joseph story presents one threat after another to God's covenant promises (e.g., Joseph's enslavement; his imprisonment; a deadly famine; Israel's departure from the the promised land), you may decide to preach Christ by way of narrative progression.

Most passages provide more than one legitimate way of preaching Christ. Let's examine the three passages I asked you to imagine preaching: the fall of Adam, the Ten Commandments, and God's famous welfare promise in Jeremiah 29:11. We'll cycle through the interchangeable lenses in our glasses in order to determine how these texts are fulfilled in Jesus.

CASE STUDY: THE FALL OF ADAM

You're preparing a sermon from Genesis 3 on the fall of Adam. How might you preach Christ from that story? In what way is it fulfilled in Jesus? Evaluate it in light of the six categories of fulfillment. Many preaching texts find their fulfillment in Christ in multiple ways, but Genesis 3 is extraordinarily rich.

Prophetic Promise. If your preaching passage extends through Genesis 3:15, you may easily preach Christ as the fulfillment of God's promise to bruise the head of the serpent. Christ is the promised offspring, who triumphs over Satan through His death (Col. 2:13–15; cf. 1 John 3:8). As many have noted, the promise in Genesis 3:15 is the first echo of the gospel in the Bible.

Ethical Instruction. Many pastors have seen in Adam and Eve's temptation a template that describes our own pattern of temptation. They preach the passage as a descriptive warning to believe God's Word over the lure of Satan's lie. Apart from the gospel, this approach to the story is sub-Christian, encouraging sanctification less by grace and more by effort. In the gospel, however, approaching the story as ethical instruction is entirely appropriate. Unlike Adam, Christ never departed from God's Word (Heb. 4:15). Therefore, in Christ, we learn to resist Satan's lie; in Christ, we can obey God's Word; in Christ, we're able to get back up after falling into sin, knowing that Jesus' blood cleanses us from all unrighteousness. The Spirit of the crucified and risen Christ gives us sanctifying grace to obey the commands of God.

Fallen Humanity. Of all the passages in Scripture that describe fallen humanity, Genesis 3 is it! Preaching this story through the lens of fallen humanity should be obvious and easy: Adam sinned, and we have sinned in Adam (Romans 5). O, how we need to be saved from ourselves! O, how we need a Savior! Jesus Christ is that Savior, who paid the penalty for our sin with His own death in our place. Exalting Jesus as the solution to sin—both Adam's and our own—would make for a gospel-rich sermon.

Typological Revelation. Though typology isn't the most conspicuous way of preaching Christ from Old Testament narratives, it should be obvious in the story of Adam. Adam is in fact a type of Christ (Rom. 5:12–19; 1 Cor. 15:21–23, 45–49). Preach Christ as the second Adam, the one in whom we have life instead of death, righteousness instead of judgment, the hope of resurrection and glory instead of eternal death and wrath. Jesus succeeded where Adam failed. If that truth doesn't inspire faith, hope, and love, nothing will.

Narrative Progression. This story stands at the headwaters of fallen humanity, posing a threat to the life of everyone born in Adam. If God's redemptive promise isn't fulfilled—if a new and greater Adam doesn't come "to make His blessings flow far as the curse is found"—all is lost. This story is a crucial part of Jesus' backstory. Adam's failure would have profoundly shaped Jesus' understanding of His own identity and mission.

Theological Theme. Genesis 3 includes multiple themes to trace to and through Jesus. To give just two examples: First, God clothing Adam and Eve with garments of skins (v. 21) suggests sacrifice, which sets the stage for sacrificial worship (Gen. 4, 8, 12, et al.), which leads to the old covenant sacrificial system (Lev. 1–7), all of which culminates in Christ's once-and-for-all sacrifice for sinners (Heb. 10:10). Second, the garden itself provides a likely background for temple imagery (1 Kings. 6:29; Ezek. 40:16), for garden references surrounding Christ's death and resurrection (John 18:1; 19:41), and for the consummated kingdom (Rev. 21–22). Other theological themes fulfilled in Christ and His kingdom are present as well, such as work and rest, curse and blessing. Genesis 3 is fertile ground for preaching Christ through the fulfillment of theological themes.

Conceivably, you *could* preach Christ all six ways in your Genesis 3 sermon. But I would caution you against it by reminding you of Eutychus, who fell asleep and tumbled to his death one night when Paul "talked still longer" (Acts 20:9). Unless you can raise people from the dead, it would be more advisable to develop one or two categories, and to set aside your other Christ-centered insights for another day. There will always be more treasures in the text than we can share.

But how do we know what to say and what to leave out? As you rely on the Spirit, you'll want to weigh several variables, such as the point of the text, the fullness of Christ, and the sharpness of the sermon. First, if the point of your text lends itself more naturally to one or two categories, follow its lead. Cut with the grain of the text. Second, if you regularly follow one or two paths of fulfillment and the text offers a less common (to you) way of preaching Christ, you may want to take that path in order to give the church a more robust vision of Christ's fullness. For example, if you rarely celebrate Christ as the fulfillment of an Old Testament type and your preaching text includes a typological revelation, then choose that path for preaching Christ. Third, if it will sharpen your sermon—if it will make your sermon more focused to highlight Christ's fulfillment in two ways instead of three, or in one way instead of two—then do that. Aim for sharpness. Our goal in preaching is to fire a bullet, not buckshot.[1]

The paths to fulfillment in Christ are many and wide. How could it be otherwise, when the Scriptures are designed to lead us to Him (John 5:39–40)? How could it be otherwise, when Jesus is so rich, so full, so deep, so glorious? Don't bypass Christ on your way to the congregation. Press into the text and touch the hem of His garment.

CASE STUDY: THE SABBATH COMMAND

The second sermon I asked you to imagine preaching was the Sabbath command (Ex. 20:8–11). How does Jesus fulfill the Sabbath command? The answer is layered with theological complexity. In his book *The Whole Christ*, Sinclair Ferguson likens it to a sort of theological litmus test for one's understanding of the law.[2] We'll wade into the law/gospel waters in Step Three, for application is where things get particularly dicey. But before we offer any contemporary application, we must work out how the Sabbath law is fulfilled in Christ.

Let's look at the Sabbath command via the six categories of fulfillment.

Prophetic Promise. This command isn't a prophetic promise, so move on to the other categories.

Narrative Progression. This command isn't given in story form, nor do we see any threat and resolution regarding a covenant promise. Move on to the other categories.

Ethical Instruction. This command, as part of covenant law, fits squarely in the category of ethical instruction. Jesus obeyed this command, and Sabbath-keeping was part of His righteousness before God.

So, whatever the command may mean for us today, you may easily preach Christ as an obedient Sabbath-keeper (Matt. 12:9; Mark 1:21; 6:2; Luke 4:16). But not only was Christ an obedient Sabbath-keeper, the Gospels depict Him also as a provocative Sabbath-clarifier (Matt. 12:1–8, 10–12; Luke 4:20–21). Jesus' actions and instructions on the Sabbath seem to indicate that He's locating the meaning of the Sabbath in Himself. This shift of significance will be of vital concern when applying the Sabbath to the church.

Fallen Humanity. Christ fulfills the Sabbath not only in His perfect Sabbath observance but also through His substitutionary death on the cross. Jesus was pierced for our transgressions, which includes Sabbath transgressions. Old covenant Israel had a pile of Sabbath transgressions, and we've only added to the pile by seeking rest outside of Christ (Matt. 11:28) and by judging others (Rom. 14:4–5). We need Jesus to save us from all our sins, including our Sabbath-breaking. And here's the good news: Jesus the Sabbath-keeper died and rose again for Sabbath-breakers like us!

Typological Revelation. Does the Sabbath function typologically? We don't have to speculate; Colossians 2:16–17 tells us plainly that it does. The Sabbath is an institution designed by God to be a predictive picture of Christ. It's a shadow of which Christ is the substance. So we're on safe ground to conclude that the rest we find in Jesus and in His coming kingdom fulfills what the Sabbath prefigured. Application to the present-day remains undeveloped, but whatever it is, it must acknowledge Christ as the fulfillment of the Sabbath.

Theological Theme. If you understand the Sabbath as a type of Christ, you'll have already dealt with several theological themes such as worship, work, and rest. Regardless of how you end up teasing out those connections for the believer's life within the new covenant, you should feel comfortable proclaiming Jesus as the one through whom and in whom we worship, work, and rest as Christians.

CASE STUDY: THE JEREMIAH PROPHECY

The well-known promise of Jeremiah 29:11 provided the text for your third sermon. How is this promise *fulfilled* in Christ? Once again, let's look at the text through the various lenses of fulfillment.

Prophetic Promise. The category of fulfillment for Jeremiah 29:11 is obvious: God's plans for the welfare of exiled Israel is a prophetic promise. Since all the promises of God find their Yes in Christ (2 Cor. 1:20), you must locate the fulfillment of this verse not in modern-day Israel, or America, or in any other nation-state but in Jesus and, by extension, those who are united to Jesus through faith. Whether Israeli or Palestinian, American or North Korean, Brazilian or Nigerian, a person receives the benefits of Jeremiah 29:11 only in Christ. Redemptive welfare doesn't exist apart from the crucified and risen Son. There is no positive future apart from the one mediator between God and men. There is no lasting hope except through our great God and Savior Jesus Christ. Preacher, preach Christ as the fulfillment of this promise.

Ethical Instruction. There's no ethical instruction in this text.

Fallen Humanity. The text doesn't highlight sin or suffering. Nevertheless, sin and suffering are present in the background as Israel is in exile due to her covenant disobedience. Which means this prophetic promise would have inspired a renewal of faith in the Lord. Despite their sin and their circumstances, God's people hadn't been abandoned by God. God still had a plan for them. Eventually, He would send His only Son to secure their eternal welfare on a blood-stained cross.

Typological Revelation. Typology may indeed be the engine that drives this prophetic promise to fulfillment. Is Jesus the embodiment of Israel? The apostles seemed to think so (e.g., Matt. 2:15 and Hos. 11:1). If this is accurate—if Israel herself was a shadow and Jesus the substance—then of course God's redemptive promises to Israel would be fulfilled in Christ, the true and greater Israel. Typological revelation may not be the best way to preach Christ from Jeremiah 29:11, but it may very well indicate how its fulfillment works.

Narrative Progression. Jeremiah 29:11 forms part of Jesus' backstory. This prophetic promise would have deepened Jesus' understanding of His mission. However, since there's no narrative tension in the text itself, narrative progression isn't the most natural way of preaching Christ in this sermon.

Theological Theme. The idea of a future hope, which Jeremiah 29:11 conveys, has a large footprint in the Bible. You'd be well-served to explore New Testament passages that show how our future hope is grounded in Jesus Christ. Tracing this theological theme will add depth to your understanding of how this verse is fulfilled in Christ.

We've methodically worked our way through each of the case studies above. In each instance, we've seen how Christ fulfills our text in multiple ways. You may have noticed how the categories, while helpful for specifying types of fulfillment, aren't as neat and tidy as they first appear. In the actual practice of interpretation, they become somewhat porous. They tend to mix together, mutually informing one another. Jeremiah 29:11 provided a good example of this. Though the text falls squarely in the category of prophetic promise, several other categories enriched our understanding of its fulfillment. Don't look at this interplay as a hermeneutical burden but as a homiletical blessing. When preaching the Old Testament, you'll never be in short supply of things to say about Jesus.

Having moved from Text to Christ, your Old Testament sermon is now well on its way to being saved. But one final step remains. You must bring the text into the lives of your listeners. In the light of Christ, you must *apply* it.

6

From Christ to Us

Place the soy sauce, olive oil, lemon juice, Worcestershire sauce, garlic powder, basil, parsley, and pepper in a blender. Add hot pepper sauce and garlic, if desired. Blend on high speed for 30 seconds until thoroughly mixed.

Pour marinade over desired type of meat. Cover, and refrigerate for up to 8 hours. Cook meat as desired.[1]

These are directions for the "Best Steak Marinade in Existence." What a spectacular recipe title! I didn't give you the ingredient measurements—you'll have to Google them for yourself. But if you're like me, you would like to try the best steak marinade in existence on the best steak in existence.

The gospel is like a marinade for the Old Testament. Every Old Testament passage we preach needs to marinate in the good news of Christ and His kingdom. Let your passage soak in the gospel. Then you'll be ready to throw the steak on the grill and get it ready for people to eat. This chapter is about *that*—about serving the meat. In other words, this chapter is about application. What good is the best marinated steak if people don't think it's been cooked for them?

STEP THREE: US

Application is the third and last step in Old Testament interpretation. You've exegeted the text in context, and you've grappled with its fulfillment in Jesus. Now you can determine how the text moves from Christ into our lives today. Now you are ready to apply the text to yourself and your hearers. But will you do so? Do you believe that application is integral to Christian preaching?

TEXT	CHRIST	US
Exegesis	Fulfillment	Application
Main Point	Gospel	Response
Jewish Sermon	Christological Sermon	Christ-Centered Sermon

APPLICATION AVERSION

Some preachers minimize the need for application. They have a condition that might be called application aversion:

- "I just preach the Word, and God does the work."
- "The Holy Spirit must drive it home. He will make the application."
- "God's Word is living and active. It won't return void. My job is just to explain the text as clearly as I can."

How can you argue with that? It's true: God works through His Word. It's also true: only the Holy Spirit can open eyes and change hearts and alter behavior. The preacher's task is to preach the Word faithfully.

Nevertheless, something is skewed in this perspective. Does faithful preaching exclude application? By no means!

God is the one who transforms people, and He can certainly do it without our help. But showing people how the gospel bears upon their lives is the normal way God brings about transformation. As the apostle Paul said, "Him we proclaim, warning everyone and teaching everyone with all wisdom, that we may present everyone mature in Christ" (Col. 1:28).

Notice a couple of things about Paul's preaching philosophy. He didn't just preach Christological sermons that exulted in the person and work of Jesus—full stop. No, preaching Christ meant *warning* and *teaching* people with *all wisdom*. Paul labored for people to see the practical implications of the gospel.

Application-averse preachers should learn from Paul's preaching philosophy. Application isn't icing on the cake, it's part of the batter. It isn't optional, it's integral. Preaching Christ without warning people and teaching them how to live is to miss the point of preaching.

To push on this issue a little harder, notice Paul's aim in preaching: *Paul's aim wasn't merely to proclaim Christ*. Now, of course, Paul *did* proclaim Christ. He *did* exult in Jesus as the fulfillment of all Scripture. He had no other way of preaching. But we mustn't confuse Paul's subject with his object. His subject was Christ, but his object was something else. His object was *people*—to *present everyone mature in Christ*. Paul championed Jesus so that people might be changed by Jesus. We should aim for the same.

Preaching is a call to action—to trust in Christ, to take up your cross and follow Christ, to treasure Christ, to be transformed in Christ. What other reason could there be for proclaiming Christ if not to see people changed by Him? The preacher must not be averse to apply the gospel, warning and teaching everyone with all wisdom that they might become mature in Christ. Application serves transformation.

APPLICATION OBSESSION

On the other hand, many contemporary preachers are *too* obsessed with application. They sense how desperately people want their lives to be improved. Week after week they preach to people whose struggles run the gamut from marital strife to the loneliness of being single, from parenting problems to infertility, from the strain of a low income to the temptations of wealth, from teenagers with acne to adults dying of cancer, from finding meaning on the job to dealing with unemployment. People are tempted to grumble, to be angry, to withhold forgiveness, to live in isolation, to give in to sexual temptation, to be proud and selfish. The list goes on and on.

Despite this dizzying array of problems, people have one thing in common: they want our preaching to help them. They want the preacher to say things that will improve their quality of life. They want to leave feeling uplifted, equipped with tools for a better life.

So the preacher feels a powerful pull to provide a quick fix—and with it comes the temptation to be simplistically relevant, immediately practical, and always down-to-earth. The more acutely he feels the pull, the more tempted he may be to adjust his content, supposing that preaching through a book of the Bible or explaining a doctrine "isn't the best way to serve people." The Old Testament in particular will seem too difficult, apart from providing fodder for illustrations or life hacks from Proverbs. Over time, such a preacher may end up resembling less the Christian pastor and more the inspirational life coach. That powerful pull he feels to improve people's lives is actually an undertow carrying him out to sea, far away from the solid ground of Christ and the gospel.

Is the solution to preach irrelevant and impractical sermons? Absolutely not! Nothing is more relevant and practical than Christ-centered exposition. Nothing is more deeply needed, relationally meaningful, and eternally significant than helping people walk with God through faith in Christ. Besides, preaching Christ doesn't mean the preacher will never talk about singleness or marriage or parenting or money or careers or health or grumbling or racism or sex or any other aspect of our human experience. But it *does* mean the preacher will never talk about these things without showing how they're connected to Jesus and the gospel.

Preaching the Old Testament, fulfilled in Christ, will lead the preacher to faithful application.

Step Three: Us

Does the gospel retain, retool, or retire the main point of the passage?

THE THREE R'S

But how? How do you make Christ-centered application from the Old Testament? How do you move from CHRIST to US? The process is straightforward: determine whether the main point of your text has been retained, retooled, or retired in Christ.

Is It Retained?

Does the gospel retain the main point of the passage? If so, the truth you're trying to convey can be applied as a response to the gospel without any modification from its Old Testament meaning. All Old Testament Scripture is profitable for Christian living, so it's little wonder that much of it comes into our lives unaltered. The covenantal context has changed but the meaning hasn't.

In the Ten Commandments, for instance, Israel is told to have no other gods before Yahweh nor to make carved images for worship

(Ex. 20:3–6). These commands remain relevant in the new covenant. The coming of Christ hasn't changed the need for us to worship God exclusively or to shun idolatry (Acts 17:19; 1 Cor. 8–10; 1 John 5:21). We can apply this Old Testament text without any alteration.

The rest of the Ten Commandments, except the Sabbath command, can be treated similarly. The application of these commands in relation to Christ remains the same as it was under the old covenant. To be sure, the new covenant highlights the depth of these commands, targeting our hearts as well as our behavior, and preachers should plumb these depths in their application. But the commands themselves remain unchanged. Christians must honor God's name and honor their parents; they must not murder, commit adultery, or steal; they must not bear false witness against a neighbor or covet his possessions (James 2:7; Eph. 6:1–4; Matt. 15:19; Rom. 13:9). These commands aren't altered in Christ; they're retained.

To shift genres, perhaps you're preaching through the book of Numbers, and you come to the dramatic story of Baal Worship at Peor (Num. 25). The opening sentence sets the stage for a sordid scene, telling us that "the people began to whore with the daughters of Moab" (v. 1). What follows is a story filled with idol worship, a deadly plague, and a preacher's kid named Phinehas who in holy zeal drives a spear through a couple having sex.

What on earth does this story have to do with our lives in Christ? How does the gospel inform its application?

Simply put, the story calls us to faith in Jesus. Like Phinehas, Jesus makes atonement for our sins, though not only for our idolatry and immorality but for all our transgressions—and not by piercing *us* but by being pierced *for us*. In addition to calling us to trust in Christ's atonement, the story also instructs us ethically. As Christians, we should avoid sexual immorality. This sin is no less a threat to the church than it was to Israel, and sexual purity is no less needed. The apostle Paul actually references the Peor incident when admonishing the Corinthians to be sexually faithful: "We must not indulge in sexual immorality as some of them did, and twenty-three thousand fell in a single day" (1 Cor. 10:8). Paul is clear: the ethical force of this Old Testament story is retained for New Testament believers. No adjustment is needed.

And so it goes throughout the Old Testament. The gospel retains a great deal of Old Testament truth "as is." The truth finds its fulfillment in Christ, and in Christ that same truth applies to our lives today. You could say these truths *resonate* with the gospel. Resonation occurs when a sound reverberates clearly and fully—and much of the Old Testament resonates with the gospel. That is, much of what the law demands, and the stories illustrate, and the prophets preach, and wisdom describes, reverberates clearly and fully in Christ. We hear the same truth without any distortion.

When the truth of an Old Testament passage is retained, you won't need to adjust it in order to apply it. Just bring the main point of the text, fulfilled in Christ, directly into the lives of your hearers.

Is It Retooled?

Sometimes you'll discern that the main point of your preaching passage isn't retained by the gospel. You can still hear the truth echoing with gospel implications, but something is different. Perhaps the sound is transposed from its original key, or you detect some distortion. The resonance isn't quite there.

When that's the case, the point of your passage is being *retooled* by the gospel. To retool something is to adapt it for improved usefulness. The gospel sometimes retools Old Testament truth. It's the same truth, but tweaked for a new day. The old covenant application has been adapted for usefulness in a new covenant era.

For example, imagine your passage highlights circumcision. You're preaching through Genesis and you come to the covenant of circumcision (Gen. 17); or you're preaching through Exodus and you reach the "bridegroom of blood" story in which Moses's wife circumcises their son (Ex. 4); or you're preaching through Joshua and your text deals with the circumcision of the entire wilderness generation (Josh. 5). In thinking about application, you recognize that the rite of circumcision is not retained in Christ. It would be wrong to apply any of these texts to the church by saying, "Abraham was circumcised; you must be circumcised." Or, "Don't you see how Moses neglected circumcision? You must not neglect circumcision." Or, "Israel couldn't enter the land without circumcision. You must be circumcised as well." Though physical circumcision was required for old covenant obedience, it isn't required for new covenant obedience (Gal. 6:15).

So how do you preach these texts? How might you apply circumcision passages in light of Christ? One way would be to generalize circumcision as an act of obedience. Though circumcision isn't required for Christians, we're called to obey all that Christ commanded. Abraham received circumcision obediently; Moses neglected it; the wilderness generation was called through it to a renewal of covenant obedience. Therefore, these texts provide us with an opportunity to challenge our listeners to obey the Lord in all He has called us to do. Our response to the gospel should be characterized by full and careful obedience (1 Cor. 7:19).

Another way to preach the circumcision passages would be to apply circumcision in light of its new covenant fulfillment. As it turns out, the heart was *always* the issue in circumcision. Moses commanded Israel to circumcise their hearts; Jeremiah and Ezekiel prophesied a new covenant in which a believer's heart would be changed; and Paul makes it plain that circumcision, in Christ, is now an inward reality of the heart, signified in baptism (Deut. 10:16; Jer. 31:33; Ezek. 36:26; Rom. 2:29; Col. 2:11–12). Application of these old covenant passages, therefore, could teach people their need for a new heart if they are to be true followers of God. Outward signs, though important, are no replacement for a heart that's alive in Christ.

So, as you come to these texts, preach about regeneration; call your people to believe in Jesus and to be baptized; highlight the Spirit's ability to do the inside-out transformation of our lives.

This process of retooling Old Testament truth according to the gospel is vital. It can also be controversial, which only underscores the need for thoughtfulness in how you move from the TEXT to CHRIST to Us.

For example, to whom do you apply texts directed to Israel? The river of God's redemptive promises flows through Israel into Christ, and through Christ to all those who are united to Him by faith. In other words, the church is now God's people. Though not identical to old covenant Israel, the church is the new covenant fulfillment of God's people in Christ. Therefore, God's promises to Israel, when modified by the gospel, do have bearing upon our lives as Christians. We are "a chosen race, a royal priesthood, a holy nation, a people for [God's] own possession" (1 Peter 2:9). So the truth about Israel, retooled in Jesus, ought to be directed *not* to everyone in general or to Americans in particular but to those who are in Christ Jesus.

Other examples of retooling include:

- **The temple**—we're no longer called to worship God in a sacred place but in a sacred way as a sacred people who are joined to the one who is the cornerstone of the new temple (Ex. 25–30; John 4:21–24; Eph. 2:19–22).
- **The Passover**—the Lord's Supper is the fulfillment of the Passover meal (Ex. 12; Luke 22:14–20).
- **The Sabbath**—old covenant Sabbath requirements may be suggestive to us today but they're not prescriptive, as our rest has come and is coming in Christ and His kingdom (Col. 2:16–17; Matt. 11:28; Heb. 4:9).
- **Warfare**—God's people still wage war today, though no longer against flesh and blood, but against spiritual forces of evil; the

Great Commission comprises our battle plan, and we leave judgment to God (1 Sam. 15:3; John 18:36; Eph. 6:10–20; Matt. 28:18–20; 2 Peter 3:7).

- **Prayer**—we must understand how the gospel reshapes old covenant prayers, like those of the Psalms, and teach the church what it means to pray them in Jesus' name (John 16:24; Eph. 2:18).

On and on we can go, but the point is this: if the gospel doesn't retain Old Testament truth, it often retools it. Never preach an Old Testament truth—about holy places or circumcision or Passover or Sabbath or Israel or warfare or prayer or anything else—without grappling with how the gospel has modified it. Pin down the modification, and you'll be ready to apply the text as Christian Scripture.

Is It Retired?

There's one other thing the gospel does to Old Testament truth. Sometimes it retires the instruction or institution altogether. That is, outside its fulfillment in Christ, no abiding application remains.

With Jesus' life, death, and resurrection, the Old Testament was fulfilled. Which means certain commands and practices were now complete. They had a long and important career, but in Christ they reached their retirement.

Obvious examples come to mind. The old covenant's dietary restrictions and food laws served an important role in marking out the people of God from the surrounding pagan nations. But with Christ's arrival, they've been fulfilled and set aside. All food is now clean because all people are now clean (Mark 7:19; Acts 10:9–15, 28). God's kingdom is no longer geographical and national, but heavenly and international. The gospel is for all the peoples of the earth.

We can say the same about old covenant sacrifices. Burnt offerings, grain offerings, peace offerings, sin offerings, guilt offerings—they've all been fulfilled in the offering of Christ's body once for all. Jesus had no need "to offer sacrifices daily, first for his own sins and then for those of the people, since he did this once for all when he offered up himself" (Heb. 7:27). The Old Testament sacrifices did their job. They had an illustrious career in the truest sense of the word—they illustrated for us the seriousness of sin and the need for a final and perfect sacrifice. But in Jesus' sacrifice, the entire sacrificial system has now been retired.

As you preach through the Old Testament, you'll come across other commands and practices that have been retired because of the gospel. Most of the so-called civil and ceremonial laws no longer play a role in the believer's life. It's not that they've been proven false; they're simply not applicable outside their original context.

But don't avoid preaching these passages! When preaching retired Old Testament truths, your sermon application should call people to embrace Jesus as the substance who has replaced the shadow, and to live in light of His finished work. When preaching the food laws, apply them to matters of holiness as a Christian, including receiving all foods as good, and eating and drinking with thanksgiving (1 Tim. 4:3–5). When preaching on the various sacrifices, call people to trust in Jesus as the final and perfect sacrifice, and to offer their own selves as living sacrifices (Rom. 12:1–2). When preaching on tithing, remind the church that temple worship, which tithing supported, has now been fulfilled in Christ, and encourage them to give generously and cheerfully in light of God's grace in Christ (2 Cor. 8–9). And so on.

The preacher who understands how the Old Testament is fulfilled in Christ will not shy away from texts in which an old covenant command or practice has been retired. Even in such texts, we can extol the finished work of Christ, the better covenant He has inaugurated, and the greater glory of living as citizens of His heavenly kingdom.

THE ASSUMPTIONS BEHIND OUR APPLICATION

We all make assumptions when applying an Old Testament text. If we assume we can transfer an Old Testament truth directly into our context without determining how the gospel affects it, then we'll find ourselves in constant error. We don't want that, and our churches don't need that. We must make sure our underlying assumptions are sound so that our application will be solid.

What underlying assumptions lead to gospel-shaped application? How can you determine whether an Old Testament truth is retained, retooled, or retired?

Assumption #1: The New Testament is paramount.

As an interpreter of God's Word, you must determine whether you'll be a left-to-right reader or a right-to-left reader. In other words, do you believe the Old Testament interprets the New Testament or that the New Testament interprets the Old?

It's a trick question. The answer is yes because the two testaments mutually interpret one another. In chapter 4, I showed that New Testament interpretation is impossible without the Old Testament. The Old Testament leans toward the New. In this sense, we must be left-to-right readers. Yet, in that same chapter, we saw that the New Testament fulfills the Old. It brings us to *the point* of the Bible—and as the point, it's paramount. Therefore, we must also be right-to-left readers. We must interpret the Old Testament in light of its fulfillment in the New.

So how do we read right-to-left? Most practically, we check our cross-references. Does the New Testament refer to our Old Testament passage? If so, how is the passage applied? Is it retained, retooled, or retired? When the New Testament applies our text, we can confidently follow its lead.

In many cases, however, there will be no New Testament quotation or allusion for us to follow. What do we do then? We practice biblical theology. That is, we trace the subject of our text through redemptive history and into the New Testament, determining how it applies in a new covenant context. What did Jesus say about the subject? What did the apostles teach? What did the early churches practice? The New Testament will never leave us without guidance about how to apply an Old Testament passage. We simply must be willing to do some careful work.

Assumption #2: Union with Christ is absolute.

Nothing inspires awe and increases my affection for Jesus like these two words: "in Christ." This little phrase (and all its variations) appears multiple times throughout the New Testament. Though its footprint is small, its theological meaning is enormous. In one passage alone (Eph. 1:3–14) we learn that:

- We were chosen in Christ before the foundation of the world.
- We were predestined for adoption as sons in Christ.
- We have received God's glorious grace in Christ.
- In Christ we have redemption through His blood.
- All things in heaven and on earth will be united in Christ.
- Our eternal inheritance is in Christ.
- Our hope is in Christ.
- We were sealed with the promised Holy Spirit in Christ.

Truly, every spiritual blessing we have comes to us in Christ. And don't misunderstand. These aren't *through-Christ* blessings, coming to us through Christ as something outside of Him. These are *in-Christ* blessings, given to us in the person of Christ Himself. In other words, we don't trust in Jesus and then receive separate blessings in addition to

Him. All God's blessings are bound up in Jesus. We receive everything from God in our union with Christ.

Consequently, union with Christ shapes our preaching application. All those prophetic promises that are Yes in Christ? In Christ, they're Yes for us, too. We receive them no other way.

All those ethical instructions that Jesus fulfilled? In Christ, God justifies us as if we ourselves fulfilled them. Outside of Jesus, there is no justification.

All the sanctifying benefits of Jesus' ethical, typological, narrative, and theological fulfillment? They come to us in Christ and Christ alone. As those in a saving relationship with God, we live and move and have our being only in union with Christ. We receive nothing from the Father apart from Him, and we can render nothing to the Father without Him. Christ is our life (Col. 3:4)!

Not to oversimplify, but application of the Old Testament can essentially be reduced to a single question: "How is this passage true for us *in Christ*?" Outside of Christ, it can have no bearing on our lives apart from condemnation. All its meaning is bound up in Him. Neglect the doctrine of union with Christ, and you'll undermine your application in every single sermon.

Assumption #3: The now/not yet tension is essential.

The kingdom of God in Christ dawned in Christ's first advent. In His life, death, resurrection, and enthronement, His kingdom was inaugurated and is now spreading throughout the world in the lives of those who trust in Jesus as Lord. Local churches are kingdom outposts, earthly embassies of the heavenly city, enjoying God's presence among themselves and extending the good news of the gospel among the nations. God's kingdom is now.

However, though the kingdom has come truly, it hasn't yet come fully. Its fullness won't be realized until Christ's second advent. When the last trumpet sounds and Jesus comes again, death will be swallowed up in the victory of resurrection, the holy city will descend from heaven, and the kingdom of the world will become "the kingdom of our Lord and of his Christ" (Rev. 11:15). Until then, the church awaits the consummation as a bride preparing herself for the bridegroom, praying for His kingdom to come on earth as it is in heaven. "Amen. Come, Lord Jesus!" (Rev. 22:20).

Grasping the *now* and *not-yet* of Christ's kingdom is essential when applying the Old Testament. If we collapse the two poles into one, problems abound. Loading all your application in the *now* leads to utopian dreams of heaven on earth, unrealistic hopes for cultural transformation, and unfounded expectations of health and wealth. This kind of over-realized preaching might be inspirational, but it inevitably creates disappointment and disillusionment. People tend to notice when the preacher's words don't come true. Where exactly is this glorious kingdom, they wonder. Is this really my best life now?

On the other hand, placing all your application in the *not-yet* doesn't fare much better. If you want to evacuate Christianity of health and vitality, then hang all of Christ's fulfillments on His second advent. Tell people that justification awaits the final judgment; give them the impression that we must "wait and see" on forgiveness; set a low expectation for God to intervene in their lives through answered prayer; reinforce the perspective that the Holy Spirit is negligibly active in our evil world. The only positive thing I can say about not-yet preaching is that it leaves room for people to be wonderfully surprised by the Lord's gracious work—despite the impression their pastor has given them! Otherwise, this kind of preaching leads to spiritual anxiety, a lack of assurance, and even a dependence on works-righteousness.

We avoid both these errors by remembering that Christ's kingdom is both now and not-yet. Whether dealing with a prophetic promise, a typological revelation, a theological theme, or another category of fulfillment, we must take care to distinguish initial fulfillment from final fulfillment. Our interpretation must not allow us to skew the application by removing the tension.

Assumption #4: The old covenant is obsolete.

It's vital to understand that Christians are no longer under the law *as a covenant.* The old covenant is obsolete, having given way to a new and better covenant in Christ (Heb. 8). The result is that we serve God "in the new way of the Spirit and not in the old way of the written code" (Rom. 7:6).

However, we're not antinomians. Though the law-as-covenant has been rendered obsolete, the laws themselves continue to shape our obedience. The Jerusalem Council, for example, when offering ethical instruction to Gentile believers, discerns worthwhile implications from laws about sacrifices, idol worship, and sexual immorality (Acts 15:28–29). Paul cites several of the Ten Commandments as exemplary of Christian love (Rom. 13:8–10). Jesus, Paul, and James each make a point of summarizing the believer's ethical life according to the law's great commandment: "You shall love your neighbor as yourself" (Mark 12:31; Gal. 5:14; James 2:8). Peter quotes from the law when encouraging Christian holiness (1 Peter 1:15–16). Though the law-as-covenant has passed away, the law-as-Scripture remains profitable for the Christian.

Some traditions divide the old covenant into moral, civil, and ceremonial categories, asserting that the so-called moral law is still in effect. Such a division of the law is ultimately unnecessary. As a covenant, none of the law remains in effect. Jesus has fulfilled it all—moral, civil, and ceremonial. But as practical instruction in ethics and wisdom, all the law remains helpful to the Christian (as is the entirety of the Old Testament). Craig Blomberg's insight should be shouted from the rooftops:

All of the Old Testament remains normative [applicable] and relevant for Jesus' followers (2 Tim 3:16), but none of it can rightly be interpreted until one understands how it has been fulfilled in Christ. Every Old Testament text must be viewed in light of Jesus' person and ministry and the changes introduced by the new covenant he inaugurated.[2]

Practically speaking, we should encourage our churches in Christian living not only through the Ten Commandments but through a Christ-centered application of all the law, including the so-called civil and ceremonial parts. This is precisely what Paul did when he uses the law about muzzling an ox to commend the payment of pastors (1 Cor. 9:9; 1 Tim. 5:18), or when he argued for non-retaliation from the law in which God says, "Vengeance is mine" (Deut. 32:35). Christians are not "under the law" (Gal. 5:18), but all the law remains useful in shaping Christian ethics, provided it is understood in light of Christ.[3] Remembering this will enable you to preach all the law, and to discern which laws have been retained, retooled, or retired.

CHRIST, OUR FILTER

Not too long ago, the city of Flint, Michigan, made the news for not having drinkable water. Water was being piped into homes from the Flint River without being sufficiently treated. The results were horrifying. Over 100,000 residents were exposed to lead contamination. Several people died. Thousands of children are expected to have serious health problems in the future. Millions of dollars and many years later, the crisis continues as the city's treatment process and plumbing infrastructure undergo replacement. Ask the people of Flint: proper water filtration is essential for a healthy life.

So is Old Testament application. Moving from an Old Testament text through fulfillment in Christ to contemporary application is a kind of filtration process. To be clear, there are no impurities in the Old Testament! Every drop of the Law, the Prophets, and the Writings is clean. The danger of contaminants comes from us. And so we must take great care to filter the text to and through Christ as carefully as we can. We want to deliver potable application to everyone who is thirsty.

Your application will be dangerous to people's spiritual health if your filtering system is dysfunctional. Therefore, don't call people to faith and obedience without having filtered the main point of your text through Jesus. Only after you determine how the person and work of Christ bears upon your text will you be ready to apply it to your hearers.

But then, after filtering everything through Jesus, turn on the faucet! Invite people to come and drink. Show them in your application how the grace of Christ can transform their lives. The salvation of your Old Testament application will be fresh water for a thirsty soul.

Part 3

What Happens
When I Preach
Christ from the
Old Testament?

7

Problems to Avoid

I've learned in pastoral ministry that solving one problem often creates another. Several years ago, our elders were concerned about the lack of intentional instruction we offered in our Sunday school ministry. In an effort to provide more focused training, we instituted a program of classes designed to lay a solid foundation in the Bible, theology, church history, and practical Christian living. The classes ran concurrently with one another, and people chose the class they wished to attend. With this new system, we accomplished our goal of intentional instruction . . . and we created a whole new problem in the process.

Previously, people were in class with one another week-in and week-out, quarter after quarter, year after year. The result was that people got to know one another through regular interactions in the Word and prayer. They noticed when someone was missing. They checked on each other and served one another. Our new structure took away this important relational element in the life of our church. It's not that we didn't foresee this potential problem, but we failed to calculate how deeply it would be felt. We resolved one problem and created another.

And guess what? The plan we devised to resolve the new problem will probably create another. Life seems to work like that.

Failing to preach Christ from the Old Testament is a serious problem. It's exegetically and theologically wrong. It dishonors Jesus as the fulfillment of Scripture and the centerpiece of salvation history. It leads people astray by perpetuating a Christless notion of the Old Testament and, worse, by inadvertently directing them to rely on God or even themselves apart from Christ.

Hopefully, this book will resolve *that* problem. But in doing so, we may open ourselves up to other problems. I've noticed at least three problems in my own preaching, as well as in the preaching of others who seek to preach gospel-centered sermons. The problems have to do with narrowness, quickness, and laziness.

FOCUSING TOO NARROWLY ON CHRIST

It's possible to focus too narrowly on Christ. How? By failing to preach Him as the second person of the Trinity. But Christ-centered preaching should be Trinity-rich preaching.

My wife's name is Natalie. When I fell in love with Natalie during college, she was all I could think about. I woke up thinking about her, went to my classes thinking about her, stumbled through my studies thinking about her, and went to bed at night thinking about her. If it sounds like I was smitten, I was! All these years later, I'm still smitten with her, though I'm happy to report that I can now give sufficient mental attention to other things in addition to her.

All that to say, it's good to be smitten with Christ. We love our Lord with an undying love (Eph. 6:24). He is our friend (John 15:15). He is our life (Col. 3:4). He is our treasure, whose surpassing worth makes every other advantage appear as garbage (Phil. 3:8). Once we understand that every jot and tittle of the Old Testament is about Him, we delight to open the Bible and preach Him to everyone who will listen.

But, like being young and in love, we can be so smitten with Christ that we have trouble thinking about anything else. If that means we forget the triune God, our preaching has become too narrow. We must not preach Christ as if the Father and the Spirit do not exist.

Sidney Greidanus cautions against hyper-focusing on Jesus to the exclusion of God the Father. He warns that we ought not preach Christ as if He alone is God. We must remember "that Christ is not to be separated from God but was sent by God, accomplished the work of God, and sought the glory of God."[1] Similarly, we must not forget "the vital role of the Holy Spirit in our salvation: regeneration, conversion, faith, sanctification."[2]

Fred Sanders echoes and amplifies Greidanus' concern. I can't recommend Sanders' book on the Trinity highly enough. In *The Deep Things of God,* Sanders encourages us to be Christ-centered without being Father-forgetful or Spirit-ignoring:

> When you declare that Jesus Christ is the center of your message, you are committing yourself to proclaim him and whatever is central to his own concerns. But Jesus himself is always centered on the work of the Father and the Spirit, so successfully focusing on Christ logically entails including the entire Trinity in that same focus. It is incoherent to hold to Jesus without simultaneously holding to the Father and the Spirit. . . . We are at all times to "[look to] Jesus, the founder and perfecter of our faith" (Heb. 12:2). But we are to look to him in a way that lets us see him situated in his relationships to the Father who sent him and the Spirit whom he sends. Unless we see Jesus in this way, we fail to see him as who he actually is.[3]

Someone might question why we should concern ourselves with the Trinity when preaching the Old Testament. But God the Trinity is there, even though we don't see Him fully revealed. More to the point, we simply don't have a Christ without a Father and a Spirit. Such a Christ does not exist. With regard to preaching Him, then, let us remember that we are preaching Him as the incarnate Son of God, beloved of the Father, full of the Spirit, the one in whom we ourselves are brought to the Father and given the Spirit.

This doesn't mean we must give the Father, the Son, and the Holy Spirit equal time in our sermons. The text and its application must determine our focus. However, if our regular preaching of Christ from the Old Testament obscures the fact that Christ has reconciled us to God as our Father, whom we now serve in the power of the Spirit, then we aren't preaching Christ as He actually is. Which is to say, we aren't truly preaching Christ at all.

Don't focus too narrowly on Christ.

MOVING TOO QUICKLY TO CHRIST

Another problem to avoid in preaching Christ from the Old Testament is moving too quickly to Christ. Like overly narrow preaching, this problem inadvertently arises from a love for Jesus and the gospel.

I mentioned being smitten with my wife. Though I was thinking about her all the time in those early months of our dating relationship, I tried not to talk about her all the time. We've all been around people who can't stop talking about the person they love. Over time, these people drift away from their friends because they're spending less time with them. Even when they're with friends, they're redirecting every conversation to their relationship.

Similarly, preachers who love Jesus want to preach Jesus. Realizing that all of Scripture is fulfilled in Him only adds fuel to this desire. But if a preacher isn't careful, he may elbow the text out of the way in order to get to Christ. Spurgeon once famously quipped that if he ever found a text "that had not got a road to Christ in it," he would "go over hedge and ditch but I would get at my Master."[4] The heart is commendable! But most people who have read Spurgeon's sermons would acknowledge that, in his love for preaching the gospel, Spurgeon could sometimes be rather loose with the text on his way to Christ.

Thankfully we can pursue powerful Christ-centered preaching *and* careful, biblical exegesis. We can have both. We'll serve our hearers well if our sermons help them see Christ in relation to the details of the passage itself.

Moving too quickly to Christ is a significant problem. It flattens the contours of God's Word, and may over time serve to undermine the gospel itself. David Helm makes this insightful but dreadful connection:

> If we preach in a way that treats the historical situation of our passage in the Old Testament as irrelevant and merely a springboard to the gospel, then we teach that the Bible is not really interested in history. History becomes a foil for theological dogma. At that point, we are only one generation away from an abstract and spiritual view of the resurrection rather than the historical view. We are one generation away from the Bible as moral mythology rather than Truth.
>
> In other words, it is entirely possible for a new breed of evangelical preachers, out of a goal of preaching Christ from all the Scriptures, to undo the very foundation of Christian preaching.[5]

Preachers and teachers, we cannot ignore this alarm. Our instinct to get to Christ is right. But we must get to Him through our passage, not in spite of it. All the Scriptures are fulfilled in Jesus. So linger in your text. Inhabit the world of your text. And though of course you may, there's no need to leave your text, even when speaking of Jesus or quoting a New Testament reference. You can preach the gospel and its fruit while remaining fully rooted in your Old Testament passage.

Don't move too quickly to Christ.

RESTING TOO LAZILY IN CHRIST

A third problem to guard against is the failure to preach the ethical implications of a text. Here's a common sermon structure among Christ-centered preachers:

- Here are the implications of the text for our lives.
- We can't live up to these implications.
- Christ has lived up to them for us.
- Let's celebrate the grace we have in Christ.

That's not a terrible sermon. It's preferable to a moralistic message that calls people to action apart from the gospel. But if this is our regular approach to preaching the Old Testament, we have a deficient understanding of what it means to preach Christ.

Don't preach Jesus Christ as a stop sign. Instead, your sermons should present Christ more like a roundabout in which, after arriving at Christ and the gospel, you circle back around to the text and apply it to people's lives. A good preacher isn't afraid to travel around the circle from TEXT to CHRIST to US multiple times throughout the sermon.

Simply put, we must not minimize the ethical implications of following Jesus. God means for the preacher to draw those implications out of the text, interpret them in light of Christ, and call people to obedience. Which means we should add another point to the all-too-common sermon structure. The additional point doesn't have to come only at the end of the sermon—it can be included as many times as the gospel is highlighted—but the logical flow is as follows:

- Here are the implications of the text for our lives.
- We can't live up to these implications.
- Christ has lived up to them for us.

- Let's celebrate the grace we have in Christ.
- Now, in Christ, let's seek to obey the implications of the text.

Obedience isn't a bad word. In fact, it's required by the Great Commission (Matt. 28:20). It's reinforced by Paul, the one who wrote that he had "decided to know nothing among you except Jesus Christ and him crucified" (1 Cor. 2:2). This is the same Paul who filled his letters to the Corinthians with instructions about leadership, sexual immorality, church discipline, lawsuits, singleness, marriage, food, idolatry, spiritual gifts, love, financial generosity, and more. For Paul, preaching "Christ and him crucified" meant preaching how to live all of life in light of the gospel. Ethical instruction flowed from gospel proclamation. Good news led to good works.

Isn't this God's intent for His Word? The things written in former days—the Old Testament—were written for our instruction (Rom. 15:4; 1 Cor. 10:11). They're profitable to us for teaching, rebuking, correcting, and training in righteousness, that we might be equipped for every good work in Christ (2 Tim. 3:15–17). In other words, the Law, the Prophets, and the Writings aren't meant to bring us to an end of ourselves so that we might rest lazily in Christ. Rather, we rest in Christ while working out our salvation, straining forward to what lies ahead, and pressing on for the prize (Phil. 2:12; 3:13–14). The Old Testament, preached in light of Christ, points to gospel-shaped living.

If you're clear with the gospel, you should never be afraid to call people to grace-fueled obedience. Any charges of legalism simply won't stick. Show people through your passage how to find rest in Christ, and make sure it's the kind of rest that propels them forward in obedience. Commend to them a lively rest, not a lazy one.

It's easy to solve one problem and create another. Unintended consequences are a part of life. They happen even when you're applying yourself to something so worthy as preaching Christ from the Old

Testament. But if you're aware of these potential problems—of focusing too narrowly on Christ, or moving too quickly to Christ, or resting too lazily in Christ—then you will be equipped to avoid them.

8

Benefits to Enjoy

What does God mean for preaching to look like? I wish I knew the definitive answer. It would have been nice for God to include in the Bible—maybe after Revelation and before the maps—an appendix for preachers. How long should a sermon be? Is a forty-minute sermon too short or too long? Are we right to think in terms of explanation, illustration, and application? Is there some component of preaching that we're overemphasizing or overlooking? Are notes in the pulpit acceptable? Speaking of pulpits, must we have them?

But God in His wisdom didn't address these details. However, the thoughtful preacher understands that the Bible's silence doesn't mean God is indifferent. On the contrary, we aim to comprehend as fully as we can those things God *has* made plain about preaching, and to allow His revelation to shape our approach as thoroughly as possible. On matters of length, structure, and delivery, we need to apply wisdom based on examples we see in Scripture, our specific preaching context, and our individual gifting in the Spirit.

But the content of preaching? That's a different story. God has spoken plainly, and there is no doubt as to what God means for the content of preaching. We are to preach the Word (2 Tim. 4:2). We are to preach the gospel (Rom. 1:15–17). We are to preach Christ (1 Cor. 1:23).

It's a good feeling to know that when you preach Christ from the Old Testament, you're preaching what God desires. It's one of the many benefits of preaching along the path of fulfillment.

For your encouragement, what follows is a list of ten benefits you'll experience as you practice Christ-centered exposition of the Old Testament. Your Old Testament sermons need to get saved, and there's much to be gained when they do.

So without further ado, in classic Letterman-style. . . .

TOP 10 BENEFITS OF PREACHING CHRIST FROM THE OLD TESTAMENT

10. A bigger Bible. Once you understand how Christ fulfills the Scriptures, you'll never again feel like two-thirds of your Bible is out-of-date or out-of-bounds for gospel preaching and Christian living.

So don't just preach the Gospels and Acts and the letters and Revelation. Preach a series through the Minor Prophets or 1 and 2 Chronicles or even—*gasp!*—Leviticus. There's nowhere you can turn in the Old Testament that isn't pointing ahead to the dawn of a new kingdom or that doesn't have the light of the gospel shining on it.

If you've felt confined to twenty-seven books of the Bible, thirty-nine more just got added to your library. Your Bible just got bigger!

9. A smaller Bible. While your Bible was busy getting bigger, it was getting smaller at the same time. You may technically have sixty-six books in which to exult in Christ. But now you also see, hopefully more clearly than ever, that the Bible truly is one book. From Genesis to Revelation, the Bible tells one story of redemption, promised in the Old Testament and fulfilled in the New.

The Old Testament points to and prepares us for Jesus. And in the fullness of time, He came.

> He was foreknown before the foundation of the world but was made manifest in the last times for the sake of you who through him are believers in God, who raised him from the dead and gave him glory, so that your faith and hope are in God (1 Peter 1:20–21).

At the center of this eternally planned and long-awaited redemption stands the Lord Jesus Christ. The entire biblical story is about Him—anticipating Him, surging toward Him, reverberating in His death and resurrection throughout the four corners of the earth, and climaxing one day in His glorious return and everlasting kingdom.

The unity of Scripture makes your Bible smaller—more concentrated, potent, and power-packed.

8. A deeper love. Over the years, my joy in Jesus has grown as I've preached Him from the Old Testament. Reading over Jesus' shoulder and pondering Him more personally has increased my sense of wonder and worship. How could your soul not be stirred, for instance, when realizing that Christ Himself would have read the Servant's speech in Isaiah 50 as His own? These verses are ours through union with Christ, but they belong to Christ first and foremost. I can't read them without being profoundly stirred:

> The Lord God has given me
> the tongue of those who are taught,
> that I may know how to sustain with a word
> him who is weary.
> Morning by morning he awakens;
> he awakens my ear

to hear as those who are taught.
The Lord God has opened my ear,
    and I was not rebellious;
    I turned not backward.
I gave my back to those who strike,
    and my cheeks to those who pull out the beard;
I hid not my face
    from disgrace and spitting.

But the Lord God helps me;
    therefore I have not been disgraced;
therefore I have set my face like a flint,
    and I know that I shall not be put to shame.
    He who vindicates me is near.
Who will contend with me?
    Let us stand up together.
Who is my adversary?
    Let him come near to me.
Behold, the Lord God helps me;
    who will declare me guilty?
Behold, all of them will wear out like a garment;
    the moth will eat them up. (vv. 4–9)

Jesus is the Servant. He would have read and prayed and been strengthened for the cross through Isaiah's words. It's marvelous to think that Jesus knows how to sustain weary people with a word; how He was taught by the Lord; how He gave Himself willingly to torture and death; how He was confident in His Father to vindicate Him over His enemies. Isaiah is describing Jesus, and his description is even more stunning when we imagine Christ Himself reading this text.

    I've come to love Jesus more through preaching Him as the

fulfillment of the Old Testament. I'm speaking autobiographically, but I'm confident that my personal experience will become your own.

7. A purer message. If the gospel is pure truth, then proclaiming it from the Old Testament is pure preaching. Sadly, however, too much Old Testament preaching is impure because it's devoid of the gospel. The -isms of our day are many: moralism, deism, materialism, nationalism, liberalism, etc. All of them pollute the gospel message. And where do most of these -isms originate? From a Christless interpretation of the Old Testament.

Learning to preach the Old Testament in light of the gospel guards the church from impure messages. When you preach Jesus, you're providing people pure spiritual milk (1 Peter 2:2). The Old Testament isn't an inspirational blog comprised of moral lessons and life principles; nor is it a magic book with incantations for health and wealth; nor is it a policy manual for civic religion. The Old Testament is the Word of God, inspired by the Spirit to reveal Christ and His kingdom. Every word will be misunderstood until the interpreter sees how the text is fulfilled in Christ.

When you preach Christ from the Old Testament, you're preaching a pure message.

6. A stouter evangelism. Another benefit of preaching Christ from the Old Testament is being able to preach evangelistically in every sermon. You don't have to be in the Gospels to talk about the gospel. You don't have to select a preaching text from Acts or the letters of Paul in order to talk about Jesus and His kingdom. Just open the Old Testament, discern how the text is marinated in the gospel, then preach Christ!

Furthermore, you'll never again need to tack Jesus onto the end of an Old Testament sermon. Whether you're in the Law, the Prophets, or the Writings, you can address unbelievers' need for Christ as you show them how Christ fulfills the text. You should have no difficulty calling them to repent and believe in response to the text itself.

As you model this kind of preaching, your church will be encouraged to invite their lost friends because they know you'll have a message for them that arises right out of the text.

5. A greater maturity. The gospel isn't just for unbelievers but also for believers. As Christians, we never move on from the gospel, only deeper into the gospel as we come to see both ourselves and Christ more clearly. Just as preaching Christ from the Old Testament gives you the opportunity to address unbelievers with the gospel in every sermon, it also gives you the privilege of preaching the gospel to believers in every sermon.

My church needs to hear the gospel and its implications every time I open the Scriptures. Your church does, too. Furthermore, they need to know their Bibles better, and preaching Christ from the Old Testament teaches them lessons they will benefit from in their own devotional reading.

God sanctifies His people through His Word. So, as we preach Jesus week in and week out, the Spirit transforms us—until one day, by God's grace, we present everyone mature in Christ (Col. 1:28). Preaching with any other focus, no matter how noble, stunts the church's growth.

4. A freer holiness. So much Old Testament preaching calls people to do, to obey, to be holy. "Be like Abraham! Don't be like Jacob! Be like Moses! Don't be like Israel! Be like David! Don't be like Ahab! Be like Esther! Don't be like Jonah! Keep the law! Turn away from evil! Honor the Lord! Pray the Psalms! Walk wisely!" None of these messages are wrong. As Christians who value the Old Testament as the Word of God, we care about holy living.

The problem isn't *that* we call people to holiness—it's *how* we call them. Holy living can only come in response to God's gracious work. God's love comes first. Always. Grace precedes law, redemption precedes obligation, freedom precedes fruitfulness.

This pattern of divine gift and human response is clearly established in the Old Testament. The introduction to the Decalogue provides one among many examples: "I am the LORD your God, who brought you out of the land of Egypt, out of the house of slavery [freedom]. You shall have no other gods before me [holiness]" (Ex. 20:2–3).

It's strangely easy to obscure this pattern when preaching from the Old Testament. But not when you preach in light of Christ! If you bring the gospel to bear upon your passage, you'll safeguard the pattern of gift and response. Your calls for holiness will ring forth within the context of Christ's fulfillment and the freedom we've been given in Him. When the gospel is the environment in which people are called to obey, duty becomes delight. Of course, there will always be Christians who abuse their freedom, using it "as a cover-up for evil" (1 Peter 2:16). But for most, reminding them of their freedom will inspire glad-hearted obedience.

3. A holier freedom. Preaching Christ from the Old Testament inspires not only a freer holiness but a holier freedom. If the emphasis of the previous benefit was on God's liberating grace, the emphasis of the present benefit is on God's constraining grace. As Christians, we aren't freed *from* holiness—we're freed *for* holiness. The God who justifies is the God who sanctifies.

Some preachers, however, celebrate grace at the expense of obedience. For them, calls for holy conduct and righteous living seem almost at odds with the freedom of justification. And so they preach the imperatives of Scripture to bring people to the indicatives of the gospel, but rarely do they reverse the current.

This approach to preaching Christ is half-true. It's true that grace should be celebrated, and that our failure in the imperatives brings us into the glory of the indicatives. But it's also true—wonderfully so—that grace flows back on its subject, empowering us to obey God's Word. The Spirit of God is the Spirit of *holiness* (Rom. 1:4). He applies to our lives the whole Bible as Christian Scripture so that we might be equipped for *every good work* (2 Tim. 3:15–17).

In other words, freedom and holiness go together, and preaching Christ from the Old Testament holds them together. Freedom always comes first—as does grace, and justification, and every other gospel indicative—but holiness follows. It's a beautiful marriage! And, what God has joined together, let not man separate.

2. A healthier church. Show me a church where the Lord Jesus Christ stands in the middle of every sermon—where the gospel is announced, acclaimed, and applied every time the Bible is open, and where people are called to love and live for the kingdom of Christ—and I'll show you a healthy church. Or, at the very least, I'll show you a church on a trajectory toward health. It cannot be otherwise. When the head of the church is honored, the body will thrive (Eph. 1:22–23).

Practically speaking, gospel doctrine creates a gospel culture within a church.[1] When the good news of Jesus fills our preaching, the gospel reverberates from the pulpit into our Sunday school classrooms, small group gatherings, personal relationships, community ministries, international missions, and everyday lives. Everything in the church begins to change because *we* begin to change. God presses the good news down into all the cracks and crevices of our lives, repairing what is broken and shaping us into the image of His Son.

1. A nobler mission. Most evangelical churches are concerned about missions. We pray, we give, and we go! But the question is: What are we exporting? What are we laboring to spread to all the peoples of the earth? It must be more than a particular worship style or discipleship strategy; it must be more than humanitarian aid in the name of

Jesus; and it must be more than merely doing missions for the sake of missions.

We must be especially wary of viewing missions as a kind of branding. Making disciples of all nations isn't about reproducing our name or our network. It isn't about exporting a look or a feel or a strategy. God has called us to a much nobler mission. To put it in Old Testament terms, our mission is:

- To see all the families of the earth blessed in Christ, who is the offspring of Abraham (Gen. 12:3).
- To bring God's sons from afar and His daughters from the ends of the earth, everyone who is called by the name of Christ (Isa. 43:6–7).
- To proclaim the death and resurrection of Jesus, the one greater than Jonah, and repentance in His name (Jonah 2–3).
- To call the nations to kiss the Son, and so live under the blessing of God's King (Ps. 2).
- To invite Rahab, Babylon, Philistia, Tyre, and Cush—Gentile enemies of God—into citizenship in the heavenly kingdom (Ps. 87).
- To declare God's glory in Christ among the nations and His marvelous works in the gospel among all the peoples (Ps. 96:3).
- To announce the ascension of the crucified and risen Son of Man, who has been given dominion and glory and a kingdom, that all peoples, nations, and languages should serve Him (Dan. 7:13–14).

On and on we could go. The Law, the Prophets, and the Writings outline for us the shape of the gospel (Luke 24:44–47). Our mission is to make disciples through the proclamation of this good news. To be sure, structures and strategies and styles play a role in the outworking of missions. But most fundamentally, our mission is a message: Jesus Christ is Lord!

- *Jesus* of Nazareth, the incarnate Son of God;
- *Christ*, the long-awaited King whose death atones for sin and whose resurrection brings life;
- *Is Lord,* so repent and believe the gospel, and enter into the blessing of His coming kingdom.

Preaching Christ from the whole Bible to the whole earth is a noble task.

The benefits of preaching Christ from the Old Testament are numerous. I've given you a Top 10 list, but I'm sure you'll find that the list can be multiplied tenfold.

Two Paintings, Two Pointings

Timothy George is the founding Dean of Beeson Divinity School. On one wall in his richly textured office hangs a painting of William Tyndale. The great sixteenth-century reformer, martyred for translating the Bible into English, is posed holding the Bible in one hand and pointing to it with the other.

On the opposite wall hangs another painting, a copy of Matthew Grünewald's depiction of the crucifixion. Juxtaposed against a black sky is the suffering Christ, crucified and dying. To the right of the cross stands John the Baptist. In one hand, John holds an open Bible, and with his other hand, he points to Jesus. The blood-red text behind John reads,

Illum oportet crescere,
Me autem minui

He must increase,
  but I must decrease.

Two paintings, two pointings. One finger toward the Bible, another toward Christ. This is the sole task of Christian preachers. We are to stand before our hearers on behalf of God with one finger pointed at the Bible and another finger pointed at Jesus. "There is no dichotomy," writes Timothy George, "between Christ and the Bible, the book and the cross.... The Bible is precious because it points us to Jesus Christ."[1]

Fellow preachers, this is why our Old Testament sermons need to get saved. Because the precious Bible points us to Jesus Christ.

Much more could be written about preaching Christ from the Old Testament. But the simple approach explained in this handbook will enable you to preach Christ more faithfully to others—and, I trust, to love Him more fully yourself.

Appendix A

Functional Questions
for Interpretation

Step One: Text

*What is the main point of the passage
in its Old Testament context?*

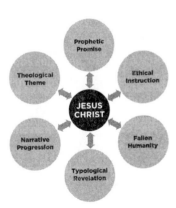

Step Two: Christ

*How is the main point of
the passage fulfilled in Christ?*

Step Three: Us

*Does the gospel retain, retool, or retire
the main point of the passage?*

Appendix B

The Hebrew Bible

THE LAW	THE PROPHETS	THE WRITINGS
Genesis	Joshua	Psalms
Exodus	Judges	Proverbs
Leviticus	1–2 Samuel	Job
Numbers	1–2 Kings[1]	Song of Solomon
Deuteronomy	Isaiah	Ruth
	Jeremiah	Lamentations
	Ezekiel	Ecclesiastes
	Hosea	Esther
	Joel	Daniel
	Amos	Ezra
	Obadiah	Nehemiah
	Jonah	1–2 Chronicles
	Micah	
	Nahum	
	Habakkuk	
	Zephaniah	
	Haggai	
	Zechariah	
	Malachi[2]	

Special Thanks

Thank you to Mark Dever and the two Garretts, Kell and Conner, who encouraged me to "write this stuff down." You said it better than that, of course, but this book wouldn't have happened without your initial nudging.

Thank you to Scott and Juliana Ruggiero for opening your beautiful Virginian home for my sabbatical. My family will never forget our time with you, as is usually the case when laughter and prayer abound ... and unexpected snow ... and one fun, old convertible.

Thank you to the book ninjas, Alex Duke and Jonathan Leeman. You guys amaze me with your big-picture insights and fine-tuning skills. I appreciate all you've done for me.

Thank you to Moody Publishers for giving me this opportunity. Drew Dyck, you made it happen. Kevin Mungons, you made it easy.

Thank you to my church family at Concord Baptist in Chattanooga, Tennessee. Your eagerness to hear the Word has given me so much room to grow as a preacher. After all these years, I'm glad you still want to listen! As Christ continues to be proclaimed among us, may we all be presented mature in Him (Col. 1:28).

Thank you to Casey, Ethan, and Amelia for cheering me on! Your excitement for Dad is more meaningful than I can put into words. You are the Jewels of Anniera.

Thank you to Natalie ... for everything. "Many women have done excellently, but you surpass them all" (Prov. 31:29).

Scripture Index

Notes

Introduction: The Rock in My Shoe

1. Haddon W. Robinson, *Biblical Preaching: The Development and Delivery of Expository Messages*, 2nd ed. (Grand Rapids: Baker, 2001), 32. Though Robinson raises the issue of Christocentrism in preaching, he does not develop the idea.
2. Sidney Greidanus, "The Necessity of Preaching Christ Also from Old Testament Texts," *Calvin Theological Journal* 34, no. 1 (1999): 191.

Chapter 1: Exegetical Necessity

1. Graeme Goldsworthy, *Gospel-Centered Hermeneutics: Foundations and Principles of Evangelical Biblical Interpretation* (Downers Grove: IVP, 2006), 48.
2. Ibid., 19.
3. The book of Psalms stands at the head of the Writings in the Hebrew Bible. Just as Jesus used Moses as a reference to the Law, here He likely uses the Psalms as a reference to the Writings. See appendix B.
4. D. A. Carson says that in John 5:39, Christ is handing us "a comprehensive hermeneutical key"—a kind of master key to the entire Old Testament (*The Gospel According to John*, Pillar New Testament Commentary [Grand Rapids: Eerdmans, 1991], 263).
5. See Part 2 of the book for a detailed explanation of how Christ fulfills the Old Testament as a whole.
6. Craig Blomberg agrees with multiple scholars when he writes that the Law and the Prophets, and sometimes just the Law, are "standard Jewish ways of referring to the entire Hebrew Scriptures." *Matthew*, The New American Commentary, vol. 22. (Nashville: Broadman, 1992), 103.
7. There is some debate about the meaning of the word "fulfilled." Matthew 5:21–48 supports the idea of Jesus clarifying the full meaning of the Old Testament, as Jesus interprets the law in a way that requires internal rather than merely external righteousness (cf. 5:20). Other uses of fulfillment language in Matthew's Gospel point to the Old Testament finding its completion in the person of Christ (1:22; 2:15, 17, 23; 4:14; 8:17; 12:17; 13:35; 21:4; 26:56; 27:9). Taken together, it is best to give "fulfilled" its fullest sense: Jesus fulfills the Old Testament by what He taught *and* by how He lived.
8. Blomberg, *Matthew*, 103–104.
9. Walter C. Kaiser, Jr., *Preaching and Teaching from the Old Testament* (Grand Rapids: Baker, 2003), 22–23.
10. Ibid., 20.

Chapter 2: Theological Necessity

1. The categories of exegesis and theology are not completely distinct. As Darrell Bock says, "Exegesis is theological, and theology should be exegetical." "Use of the Old Testament in the New," in *Foundations for Biblical Interpretation*, ed. David S. Dockery, Kenneth A. Mathews, and Robert B. Sloan (Nashville: Broadman, 1994), 108.

2. Edmund P. Clowney, *Preaching and Biblical Theology* (Grand Rapids: Eerdmans, 1961), 15.

3. William L. Lane, *Hebrews 1–8,* Word Bible Commentary, vol. 47a (Dallas: Word, 1991), 10–11.

4. Peter J. Gentry and Stephen J. Wellum, *Kingdom Through Covenant* (Wheaton: Crossway, 2012), 138. The table called "The Riverbanks of Redemptive History" is adapted from Gentry and Wellum's Table 4.1, 135.

5. George H. Guthrie, *Hebrews,* NIV Application Commentary (Grand Rapids: Zondervan, 1998), 282.

6. Philip Edgcumbe Hughes, *Paul's Second Epistle to the Corinthians*, New International Commentary on the New Testament (Grand Rapids: Eerdmans, 1962), 112.

7. A paraphrase from John Piper's *The Supremacy of God in Preaching* (Grand Rapids: Baker, 1990), 20: "Then when preaching takes up the ordinary things of life . . . these matters are not only taken up. They are taken all the way up into God."

Chapter 3: The Preaching Text

1. Quoted in David G. McCullough, *Brave Companions: Portraits in History* (New York: Prentice Hall, 1992), 89. All subsequent information on the Panama Railroad is taken from McCullough's chapter "Steam Road to El Dorado," 89–104.

2. Ibid., 90.

3. Graeme Goldsworthy, *Gospel-Centered Hermeneutics: Foundations and Principles of Evangelical Biblical Interpretation* (Downers Grove: IVP, 2006), 251.

4. Sidney Greidanus, *The Modern Preacher and the Ancient Text: Interpreting and Preaching Biblical Literature* (Grand Rapids: Eerdmans, 1988), 126.

5. Mark Dever and Greg Gilbert elaborate on this approach to preaching in a unique and helpful chapter, "What to Preach On," *Preach: Theology Meets Practice* (Nashville: Broadman & Holman, 2012), 63–78.

Chapter 4: Fulfillment in Christ

1. Quoted in the Foreword to Tony Merida's helpful book on preaching, *The Christ-Centered Expositor: A Field Guide for Word-Driven Disciple Makers* (Nashville: Broadman & Holman, 2016).

2. Christopher J. H. Wright, *Knowing Jesus Through the Old Testament* (Downers Grove: IVP, 1992), ix.

3. Bryan Chapell, *Christ-Centered Preaching: Redeeming the Expository Sermon* (Grand Rapids: Baker, 1994), 271.

4. David Murray, *Jesus on Every Page: 10 Simple Ways to Seek and Find Christ in the Old Testament* (Nashville: Thomas Nelson, 2013), 136. Murray's definition

also rightly includes types of Jesus' enemies, but I'm limiting our focus to types of Christ.

5. Ibid., 138.
6. I'm indebted to Stephen Wellum for pressing the need for biblical warrant in typology, and to Dennis Johnson for his careful work in establishing biblical warrant. The image of cross-reference strata belongs to Johnson. See *Him We Proclaim: Preaching Christ from All the Scriptures* (Phillipsburg: P&R Publishing, 2007), 199–217.

Chapter 5: Case Studies in Fulfillment

1. Haddon W. Robinson, *Biblical Preaching: The Development and Delivery of Expository Messages*, 2nd ed. (Grand Rapids: Baker, 2001), 35.
2. Sinclair Ferguson, *The Whole Christ: Legalism, Antinomianism, and Gospel Assurance—Why the Marrow Controversy Still Matters* (Wheaton: Crossway, 2016), 143–44, n. 17.

Chapter 6: From Christ to Us

1. "Best Steak Marinade in Existence," Allrecipes, https://www.allrecipes.com/recipe/143809/best-steak-marinade-in-existence/.
2. Craig Blomberg, *Matthew*, The New American Commentary, vol. 22. (Nashville: Broadman, 1992), 103–104.
3. See Brian Rosner's *Paul and the Law: Keeping the Commandments of God* (Downers Grove: IVP, 2013) for a detailed defense of the view sketched here.

Chapter 7: Problems to Avoid

1. Sidney Greidanus, *Preaching Christ from the Old Testament* (Grand Rapids: Eerdmans, 1999), 179.
2. Ibid., 182.
3. Fred Sanders, *The Deep Things of God: How the Trinity Changes Everything* (Wheaton: Crossway, 2010), 168–69.
4. Charles Spurgeon, "Christ Precious to Believers," *The Metropolitan Tabernacle Pulpit*, sermon delivered March 30, 1890, Metropolitan Tabernacle, Newington, Spurgeon Gems, https://www.spurgeongems.org/vols34-36/chs2137.pdf.
5. David Helm, *Expositional Preaching: How We Speak God's Word Today* (Wheaton: Crossway, 2014), 65.

Chapter 8: Benefits to Enjoy

1. For an unparalleled description of a gospel culture within a church, see Ray Ortland's *The Gospel: How the Church Portrays the Beauty of Christ* (Wheaton: Crossway, 2014).

Conclusion: Two Paintings, Two Pointings

1. Timothy George, "Between Two Paintings," *JBDS* 1 (2006): 1. The clever play on words (paintings/pointings) is George's. The two paintings are *Crucifixion* (Matthias Grünewald, ca. 1480–1528; a panel for the Isenheim Altarpiece, St. Anthony's monastery; currently displayed at Unterlinden Museum at Colmar,

France), and *William Tyndale* (unknown artist, late 17th or early 18th century, Hertford College, Oxford).

Appendix B: The Hebrew Bible

1. The books of Joshua through 2 Kings are considered the Former Prophets.
2. The books of Isaiah through Malachi are considered the Latter Prophets.

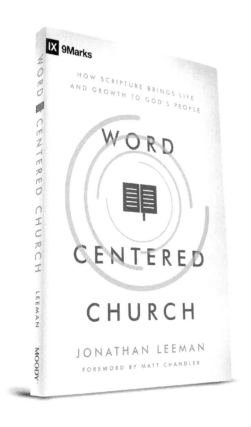

Pastor, it's time to turn down the noise and focus on what matters.

DON'T JUST EXPLAIN THE BIBLE.
LET YOUR PEOPLE FEEL ITS PASSION.

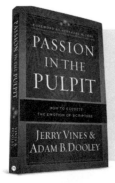

Jerry Vines and Adam Dooley teach you how to exegete not only the verbal content of Scripture but also its emotional appeal. Learn the exegetical steps to discern the pathos of your text. Master the verbal, vocal, and visual techniques to communicate it with power and emotion. And start preaching not only to your people's minds but also to their hearts.

978-0-8024-1838-8

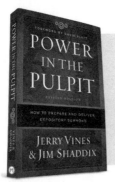

Is powerful preaching the responsibility of the pastor or a gift from the Holy Spirit? This practical volume will help pastors achieve a balance between preparation and inspiration. Blending the perspectives of two experienced pastors, this resource is indispensable for every expository preacher.

978-0-8024-1557-8

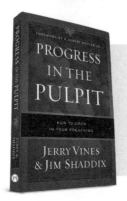

While most preaching books are geared toward new preachers, *Progress in the Pulpit* builds on the basics and focuses on aspects of preaching that often fall into neglect. It also gives special attention to some of the latest cultural and homiletical trends that many pastors don't have time to research on their own.

978-0-8024-1530-1

WHAT EVERY PASTOR NEEDS: MORE TIME FOR MINISTRY.

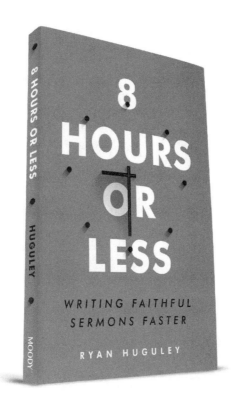